"There is no country where the energetic man can, by his own labor, and by his own industry, ingenuity, and frugality, acquire competency as he can in America."

ULYSSES S. GRANT

U. S. GRANT ALBUM ★★★★★

A PICTORIAL BIOGRAPHY OF ULYSSES S. GRANT
From Leather Clerk to the White House

By
Lawrence A. Frost

U. S. GRANT PORTRAIT—This oil painting by Mrs. Darragh of Philadelphia was presented to the United States Military Academy by Mrs. George W. Shields. Made from a photograph by Gutekunst of Philadelphia in 1865 and selected by Mrs. Grant the finished painting was hung in Grant Hall at the Academy. Courtesy West Point Museum Collections.

BONANZA BOOKS - NEW YORK

COPYRIGHT © MCMLXVI BY SUPERIOR PUBLISHING COMPANY, SEATTLE, WASHINGTON

Library of Congress Card Catalogue number 66-25419

All rights reserved

This edition published by Bonanza Books,
a division of Crown Publishers, Inc.,
by arrangement with Superior Publishing Company
a b c d e f g h

PRINTED IN THE UNITED STATES OF AMERICA

Dedication

To My Mother and
My Father.

CONTENTS

Author's Preface

To some this volume may appear to over-emphasize the military aspect of Grant's life and not provide enough of the political portion. Though Grant made important political contributions they did not compare in importance with those of his military career.

His life was one filled with frustration and failure, good fortune and success. To say that he earned his early success would be an unfair appraisal; later, he did—yet that would have been impossible had he not had the early opportunities that built the foundation for his later successes.

A character analysis several years before the Civil War would have indicated that he was unfit for and had no interest in leading an army. In like manner he was not cut out to be a merchant, salesman or farmer, though he had a great love for the latter. Slow-moving, lethargic, introverted, modest, with little ego and a firm resolve not to push his own interests or ideas, he gave no evidence of ambition or desire for position. Excessively interested in men of wealth, he had no abilities in the art of fortune making.

He was a great believer in Fate—it was his destiny to be at the right place at the right time. Yet one cannot overlook certain attributes that stood him in good stead when he was tested—his calm and unemotional nature, his loyalty, honesty and his courage.

Had he been a Southerner with the same parents, personality, training and experience, and then exchanged places with Lee while both commanded an army, would he have led the South to victory?

Grant's mainstay was his continuous pounding of his enemy and this could procure victory only by a preponderance of men and supplies—something the South did not have and would never have. It was Grant's and the North's good fortune he was born where he was.

In no way can this subtract from Grant's greatness as a military leader, but it is interesting for those who deal with supposition.

There is no question that Grant was a political misfit, and certainly not the first or the last to hold high office. His party as they often do, selected him because of his ability to get votes and put them back into power. Not once did they consider his ability to hold office, nor did they wish to. In spite of his party's lack of concern for their country's well-being, he did surprisingly well ill-equipped as he was to meet the challenges before him.

Though his political supporters suggested a third term, his heart was not in it. What had distressed him most was to have been deceived by those he had trusted.

This Civil War hero had given all that he could when called upon by his country in time of war and peace. It was his misfortune to accept the Presidency at a time that would have been difficult for an accomplished statesman. Yet he did his best.

His world travels had restored his confidence and composure only for him to meet financial reverses in an ill-chosen investment. Beaten and buffeted toward the last, and stricken with a fatal malignancy, this old warrior refused to recognize defeat. His time had come—a fact he accepted with stoic calm—so he grasped at the last chance to show his great devotion to his wife and children. He wrote his *Memoirs*, laboring over them many months after his voice had failed him, when lesser men would have given up. He left them this legacy of love, completed just one week before he passed away.   L.A.F.

GRANT IN PEACE—An engraving by A. B. Walter that enjoyed a nationwide sale at the end of the war.

8

Chapter One

Tanbark Feeds a Family

Jesse Root Grant had a burning desire to succeed. His father Noah, retiring from the Continental Army as a captain, had restless feet and a liking for liquor. Breaking up his home after the death of his second wife, Jesse's mother, Noah farmed out the children, leaving Jesse with the family of an Ohio Supreme Court Justice, George Tod. Though Jesse worked hard, it was here he was given some love, education and inspiration. In 1810, at age 16, he struck off for Maysville, Kentucky, to apprentice himself in his half-brother Peter's tannery. Here he worked for five hard years, using every evening to read. He knew he needed knowledge to succeed.

Jesse Grant had mapped a route through life at the age of 15. At 25 he reached the first milestone. His obligation to Peter paid by his 21st birthday, he worked into a partnership with the tanner John F. Wells at Ravenna, Ohio. His half interest, worth $1,500, was a realization that he had fulfilled his expectation for himself by the age of 25. The next milestone would be the acquisiton of a wife.

An untimely malarial epidemic struck Ravenna. Jesse was one of its victims, and his romance with Prudence Hall was severed. Ill for a year and unable to work, he lost his share in the business and acquired some indebtedness. The first six months of 1820 were spent convalescing at Peter's home. In June he crossed the river onto the Ohio shore to visit Point Pleasant. Thomas Page was opening a tannery in the village and needed a tanner. Jesse got the job.

Inland trips to purchase hides soon led him to the door of John Simpson's brick home, for here lived two attractive, marriageable daughters. The Simpsons were a respectable family of moderate means, their 600 acre farm being a credit to them.

Hannah Simpson was considered handsome—her older sister, Mary, pretty—but the quietness of Hannah appealed to the noisy, talkative Jesse. By early 1821 his intentions were obvious to the tall, graceful girl. He had been doing well at the tannery. And his eccentricities covered a gentle and affectionate disposition along with his characteristic energy and ambition.

Hannah, who would be 23 on November 23, 1821, married Jesse in her father's house on June 24, 1821. Housekeeping at Point Pleasant began next door to the tannery.

The six foot Jesse now had inspiration. Previously his duties as a foreman at the tannery

ULYSSES GRANT'S FATHER—Jesse Root Grant loved to talk, argue, make speeches, write rhymes for the local newspaper emphasizing his strong opinions. A six-footer, he was very ambitious and energetic. When visiting Washington he would stay at a hotel rather than at the White House where he would get into violent arguments with Ulysses' father-in-law Colonel Dent. Courtesy Library of Congress.

had occupied his full attention. Now, with a wife who doubled the pleasure of his successes and absorbed a portion of the sting from his defeats, he could plan for the next milestone.

On April 27, 1822, a son was born. Naming the 10 3/4 pound child became a family affair that went into a second month. At the final discussion, Hannah held for "Albert"—a choice that was supported by her sister Mary. Her other sister, Anne, liked the sound of "Theodore."

Jesse, for once, said little, and demonstrated tact and shrewdness. He had lent Hannah's mother one of his favorite books, Fenelon's *Telemachus*, for he knew she loved good reading. He admired the character "Ulysses, the great Grecian general who defeated the Trojans by the strategy of the wooden horse." And so did Mrs. Simpson.

The decision of a name was to be made on a ballot vote dropped into a hat. The youngest present, 17 year old Anne, did the drawing. The tally showed: Ulysses 2, Albert 2, Theodore 1 and Hiram 1. With this conclusion, Jesse prudently announced that the boy would be named "Hiram Ulysses." Between Jesse and Grandmother Simpson the growing lad answered to "Ulysses," the family and neighbors soon contracting it to "Lyss."

The next milestone had to be a tannery, for Jesse and Hannah had saved $1,100 by 1823 and paid off all his debts. The village of Georgetown, 25 miles to the east of Point Pleasant, seemed a logical site. A growing community, being the seat of Brown County, it was surrounded by an adequate supply of oak trees.

Jesse bought a lot for $50 before Justice of the Peace Thomas L. Hamer, a factor that may have had much to do with the origin of their long friendship. The site of the new tannery 300 feet east of the town square was across the road from the two-story brick home he built and moved his family into during the fall of 1823.

Lyss displayed an early liking for horses. Near his second birthday he was taken to a traveling one-ring circus. The concluding act was that of a trained pony. When the ringmaster cried out: "Who will ride the pony?" Lyss persisted in his begging until his father held him on the pony's back for several trips around the ring. His glee was in evidence at every step.

Lyss loved horses and they seemed to love him. The little fellow enjoyed playing in their occupied stalls or under the bellies of the strange teams that stood at the tannery gate. Their swishing tails—for the tannery was a breeding place for flies—frequently tempted him to swing on them. Both neighbors and visitors, becoming alarmed at the proximity of the lad to the iron-shod hoofs, would hurry to Hannah with the story. After listening patiently to the oft repeated report she would reply: "Horses seem to understand Ulysses."

His love for horses was evident by the frequency with which he was seen holding the teams for the various drivers around the tannery. And his prideful father enjoyed watching him stand on the bare backs of his work horses as he drove them to the nearby stream for water.

A second son became the next milestone for Jesse. Born September 23, 1825, he was named Samuel Simpson after Hannah's brother. This necessitated the construction of a small addition to the house.

The only school at the time was a subscription school. Each parent subscribed from $1.50 to $2 a child for the thirteen week period. If cash was not available an equivalent in wheat, corn or tobacco was provided. The teacher, usually an Easterner, pounded the three R's into a single roomful of pupils ranging from five to twenty-one years of age. Attention was maintained by the frequent application of beechwood switches, an approach that astonished young Lyss since his parents never had licked or scolded him.

Jesse recalled later that Lyss started going to school around the age of four while Lyss remembered it to have been around five or six. Jesse also recalled that he had been quite a student. Ulysses did not think of himself in that fashion; rather that he "was not studious in habit." He displayed no evidence of genius, though Jesse thought otherwise.

He played well with his classmates at school but preferred riding and handling horses. Marbles, swimming, snowball fights, skating and sledding were the sports he most enjoyed.

Georgetown was proving to be an excellent location for the Grant tanyard. Jesse had purchased a fifty-acre oak forest just a mile away to insure a supply of tanbark. Opening up a butchering business insured a constant supply of hides. With the increase of business it was necessary to enlarge his tanyard and add more men and horses. In slack periods men could be laid off. The horses were kept busy plowing or in general delivery. It was natural enough to branch into the livery business, carrying passengers around the village or to nearby towns.

In his early years, Jesse had little time for church. Of English Puritan lineage, he had been given a solid Christian background. Hannah's influence brought him to her Methodist church where he became a "ruling spirit in church affairs." Whatever Jesse did he did with all his heart and energy. And so it was when he succeeded attorney Tom Hamer as master of the Georgetown Masonic Lodge No. 72. His love of argument, since he held strong opinions, found an outlet in the opportunities to make speeches. With his definite pro-Northern opinions oft-expressed in a community predominantly composed of Southerners, there were times when his presence was resented. His great energy had to be expended; when he couldn't make speeches, he sought other outlets for his views. Letters to the editor, sometimes in rhyme, was one means.

Though most every family in Brown County owned a horse and every family member was expected to know how to handle one, Lyss was showing unusual aptitude. In the fall of 1829, Jesse

had driven to Ripley, some 12 miles away, for the day. Young Lyss harnessed a three-year-old colt that had been broken only to the saddle, hitching him to a sled. All day he hauled load after load of brush home until he had a pile as large as a cabin. Jesse fairly burst with pride when he arrived home that evening and saw the results of that unrequested labor of his seven-year-old son.

About this time Lyss had a playmate several years older than himself, Dan Ammen, who saved his life. While seated on a poplar log fishing, Lyss fell into the fast-flowing, muddy water. Young Ammen ran downstream to an overhanging willow from which he fortunately grabbed Lyss as he surfaced. In later years, while President, he would tell Dan that he was to blame for all the troubles Grant had inherited. By saving his life Ammen had eliminated Grant's chances of happiness.

ULYSSES GRANT'S MOTHER—Hannah Simpson Grant never boasted, argued, gossiped or praised, believing that you should praise the Lord for giving you the opportunity. She said little and displayed no emotion. Jesse said of her: "Her steadiness and strength of character have been the stay of the family through life." Though she lived until May 11, 1883, she never visited the White House.

BIRTHPLACE OF U. S. GRANT—This two-room cottage at Point Pleasant, Ohio, a stone's-throw from the Ohio River, was the scene of Ulysses' birth April 27, 1822. The 16x19 feet frame building was a traveling exhibit on a river towboat for a decade prior to 1896 then stood in a glass case at the Ohio State Fair Grounds in Columbus, in a glass shelter. After an absence from Point Pleasant for more than 50 years, it was returned and preserved by the Ohio Historical Society. Courtesy Ohio Historical Society.

At the age of eight he broke bark. Using a mall, he pounded the two and three-foot slabs of bark hauled from the woods into chunks four or five inches long, then placed them in the hopper of the grinding mill. Lyss would evade this assignment at every opportunity by driving the team attached to the circling sweep that turned the huge coffeemill-like grinder. He would drive the teams to the woods for loads of bark piled on the wagon or unloaded by Jesse's men, but to scrape or otherwise touch the hides was repulsive to him. Always was he to detest the sight of blood, a principal reason why he would never hunt with the other boys. He could not bear to see an animal suffer or die.

By the time he was 10 he drove a load of leather to Cincinnati, bringing back several passengers to Georgetown. He had driven passengers to Ripley, Maysville, Higginsport and West Union earning enough to buy a horse. His mother had admonished him to "be sure you don't became *Useless.*" In his father's eyes he was not, for the story is told that he drove two lawyers up to Toledo, Michigan Territory, over 200 miles away.

Hannah Grant was a quiet sort, unemotional and not easily disturbed. Each day was one of labor and responsibilities. She was devoted to her

GRANT RESIDENCE AND TANNERY AT BETHEL, OHIO—Jesse Grant had formed a partnership with E. A. Collins, a tanner at Bethel, about 1845. Tannery is in the foreground; the Grant residence is on the right. Courtesy Library of Congress.

family and to her church, and though her lot was not easy, she had a comfortable home and was well provided for. But her family was growing. Her first daughter, Clara, was born December 11, 1828. Virginia was born February 20, 1832, Orvil L., May 15, 1835, and Mary Frances July 20, 1839.

Lyss' mother said little but made a profound and lasting impression upon him. Neither she nor Jesse ever scolded or punished. He always remembered, and followed to the point of superstition, her advice that "once having put a hand to the plough one can neither look or turn back." If he would miss a turn in the road he would not turn back but would "go on until a road was found turning in the right direction, take that, and come in by the other side." This firmly imbedded characteristic became an obsession with him during his remaining years.

Circuses broke up the monotony of summer labors. And to Lyss they provided an opportunity to observe the equestrian acts. On one such occasion when accepting the ringmaster's challenge to ride the trick horse and win five dollars, he studied the large, fat animal and concluded he could do it by locking his arms around its neck. He won the five dollars. On another occasion he weathered the wheeling, bucking and sudden stops of the trick horse, showing no emotion when the ringmaster tossed a large monkey on his back that pulled his air and scratched him.

At age nine he had developed the faculty of breaking a horse to pace. In several hours, sometimes one, he could break a neighbor's colt to pace. His ability to break, train and ride horses became known over a large area, and by the time he was 15 he had established the reputation of being the best horseman in southern Ohio.

When he was eight Lyss fell in love with the colt of a farmer, Robert Ralston. Appearing with it at the tannery one day, Ralston offered to sell for 25 dollars; Jesse countered with an offer of 20. Lyss begged so vigorously he was permitted to go after the horse. His father told him the colt was worth no more than 20 dollars, but if Ralston wouldn't take that to offer him 22 1/2, and if he wouldn't take that to offer him 25. When the young horse trader arrived at the Ralston farm he said to him: "Papa says I may offer you $20 for the colt, but if you won't take that to offer 22 1/2, and if you won't take that to give you 25." Years later he wrote that he showed quite plainly he had come for the colt.

Lyss continued attending the Georgetown school during the winter sessions. There were no real intimacies or enemies during these years. Perhaps his only close friend had been Dan Ammen, two years his senior. And there were no youthful love affairs for he had been rather shy around girls. The only fight that can be recalled was with a bigger boy who was somewhat of a bully, and who had tormented him beyond endurance.

Average in geography, grammer and spelling, he was unusually good in arithmetic. Though many problems were given for working out on a slate, mental arithmetic was quite the vogue and teachers enjoyed calling out the problems so students could work them in their heads. In both Lyss excelled, being considered somewhat of a rapid calculator.

His father had visions of higher education for Ulysses, higher than could be obtained in Georgetown. At the age of 14 he was sent across the Ohio River to attend Richeson's and Rand's *Maysville Seminary*. There in Maysville, Kentucky, his Aunt Pamelia, Peter Grant's widow, could keep an eye upon him. In the fall of 1838 he attended the *Presbyterian Academy* of Ripley, Ohio, boarding with a tanner. Unkown to him his father was investigating the possibility of sending him to West Point, though he had shown no military interest. In school he was an average student, was not quarrelsome, had no bad habits. He was inquisitive about the opinions of others, asking many questions, and always carried a stick on which he whittled a great deal but never made anything.

Just before he entered school that year his father, suffering a labor shortage, asked him to work in the beam room. He agreed to but frankly stated that tanning was not for him. He said he would

GRANT TANNERY AT POINT PLEASANT, OHIO—It was next door to the one-story frame house Jesse rented from Lee Thompson. Courtesy Ohio Historical Society.

work in the tannery until he was 21 but not a day longer. Jesse, wise father that he was, told him he did not want him to work at anything he disliked so much. The subject of West Point was discussed several months later.

In his *Memoirs* Ulysses wrote: "I detested the trade (tanning), preferring almost any other labor; but I was fond of agriculture, and of all employment in which horses were used . . . . From . . . 11 until 17 I did all the work done with horses, such as breaking up the land, furrowing, plowing corn and potatoes, bringing in the crops when harvested, hauling all the wood, besides tending two or three horses, a cow or two, and sawing wood for stoves, etc., while attending school. For this I was compensated by the fact that there never was any scolding or punishment by my parents." And of his schooling he wrote: "I was not studious in habit, and probably did not progress enough to compensate for the outlay for board and tuition."

JESSE GRANT RESIDENCE IN GEORGETOWN, OHIO—It still stands on the corner of Grant and Water Streets. In the distance on the right may be seen the tower of the Brown County courthouse. The Grant tannery was to the left. Courtesy Ohio Historical Society.

Chapter Two

Classmates Called Him Sam

Representative Thomas L. Hamer and Jesse Grant had not been on speaking terms since 1833. In the fall of that year they had taken sides on a policy of President Jackson's. Grant thought Jackson incautious in withdrawing funds from the federal bank; Hamer felt otherwise, for he idolized Jackson. The quarrel led to a severance of the long, firm friendship. Neither would attempt reconciliation.

Henry Clay of Kentucky, leader of the new Whig party, had excited Jesse to the point that he drew away from the Democratic party he always had supported. When Clay failed to get the nomination in 1836, he stayed away from the polls rather than vote against the Democratic ticket.

In the fall of 1838 he had written to his friend Senator Thomas Morris seeking an appointment to West Point for his son. Morris had none available but advised him to write to the War Department since there was a vacancy in the Fifth Congressional District of Ohio. This Jesse did. On learning that a vacancy had occurred, because his physician Dr. Bailey's son Bart was dropped from the Military Academy for several improprieties there, he told Ulysses that he thought he was going to receive the appointment.

"What appointment?"

"To West Point. I have applied for it."

"But I won't go!"

And as Ulysses recalled later: "He said he thought I would, *and I thought so too, if he did.*"

Willing to put his pride aside where his first born was concerned, there was nothing else that Jesse could do but write to Tom Hamer. Addressing a letter to him on February 19, 1839, he asked for assistance in obtaining an appointment for Ulysses.

Tom Hamer seized the opportunity to end the old difference. Filling out the necessary application papers for the War Department, he wrote "Ulysses S. Grant," thinking Ulysses carried in the middle his mother's family name of "Simpson." Hamer had forgotten or had not known that the first name was Hiram.

The Military Academy was limited to 250 cadets, a candidate being appointed by the Representative of each Congressional District, the President being permitted to appoint ten at large. The admission age was 16 to 21 and the minimum height was five feet. Ulysses at 17 was five feet one inch and weighed 117 pounds. The number summoned to appear for

BRIGADIER GENERAL THOMAS L. HAMER—Serving six years as a member of Congress, attorney Hamer died of disease near Monterey during the war with Mexico. It was he who appointed Ulysses to West Point and caused a mixup in his name. Courtesy Ohio Historical Society.

behind the nickname "Useless" was no benefit if he was to assume another more painful one such as "Hug." Rearrangement to appear "U.H.G." was the solution. He found it necessary to transpose his first two names when, on May 29, 1839, he signed the Adjutant's register, "Ulysses Hiram Grant." This did not solve all of his difficulty with his name, however.

Adjutant George Waggaman had no appointment there for Ulysses Hiram Grant on his official list from the War Department. He did have one for Elihu Grant from New York—oh yes, and one for a Ulysses S. Grant from Ohio. Explaining that his Congressman had erred in making out the papers made little difference. The name on the official list, he was advised, could not be changed except by the War Department. If he was to enter the Military Academy, it must be by the name Representative Hamer had used on the official application.

He had traveled far to be a cadet. There was only one way left to be one—assume the new name.

COMMODORE DANIEL AMMEN—A lifetime friend of Ulysses, he saved him from drowning in the White Oak Creek of Brown County near Georgetown, Ohio. Courtesy Library of Congress.

the preliminary examination in June of 1839 was 76, 13 of whom were named by the President. Only half of these would graduate four years later.

By the middle of May he was ready to leave. He had made the round of visits to his relatives with a light heart, for he did not expect to be gone long. Though he had no liking for a military education, he was looking forward to the trip that would carry him to it. He suspected he would not be able to pass the entrance examination and would soon be home. This trip, that permitted stopovers in Philadelphia and New York, might not have been so enjoyable had he known that he would pass the examination without difficulty.

His family had given him a trunk. On it in large, brass tacks were his initials, H.U.G. (for Hiram Ulysses Grant). This would not do. Leaving

I, Cadet U. S. Grant, of the State of Ohio, aged seventeen years and two months, do hereby engage, with the consent of my guardian, to serve in the Army of the United States for eight years, unless sooner discharged by the proper authority. And I, Cadet U. S. Grant, do hereby pledge my word of honor as a gentleman, that I will faithfully observe the Rules and Articles of War, the Regulations for the Military Academy; and that I will in like manner, observe and obey the orders of the President of the United States, and the orders of the officers appointed over me, according to the rules and discipline of War.

Subscribed to at West Point, N.Y., this 10th. day of September eighteen hundred and thirty nine, in presence of

TO SERVE FOR EIGHT YEARS—
Cadet U. S. Grant agrees to serve in the U. S. Army until age 25. Courtesy United States Military Academy Archives.

Word of the incident got around fast, and was confirmed when the lists were posted on the North Barracks' bulletin board. With the initials "U.S." in the hands of the second year men eager for some fun, he couldn't be anyone other than "United States Grant" or "Uncle Sam Grant." So "Uncle Sam" he became, and later, plain "Sam."

Sam was not prepossessing in appearance. Though compactly built he was stoop-shouldered and unmilitary in appearance, with a clumsy, plowed-field gait. From the first he gathered demerits for slovenly dress, and for oversleeping.

It was an uncomfortable, unpleasant way of life. From five in the morning until ten each night he moved to the roll of drums and the commands of his superiors. Never seeming to do things right in this new world, he was the recipient of demerits for infractions of the numerous regulations that governed the cadets, or was being punished by upper classmen for failing to observe the stringent rules they imposed on first year men.

His classmates saw him as a self-reliant, unselfish, pure-minded, even-tempered individual, who endured the abuse heaped upon him and escaped much of the hazing because of an obliging nature and a quiet disposition.

The first ten weeks were the hardest, for those were the weeks before the academic studies began in September. It was during this time that the raw youths were put through a basic training that toughened and trained their bodies and minds. With this period concluded Sam was priviliged to see "the two men most to be envied in the nation," Cadet Commandant Captain Charles F. Smith and General of the Army Winfield Scott.

Smith, tall, straight, mustachioed and every inch a soldier in appearance, was the Cadet Corps' idol. Scott, or "Old Fuss and Feathers" as he was called, was a splendid male specimen, six-foot-four, a hero of the War of 1812 and a magnificent figure as he moved around in his dazzling uniform. This had been worth the trip. Even President Martin Van Buren's visit to West Point the next summer did not impress him as much.

With the beginning of the classes Sam soon found that mathematics was to be his favorite. Though he had shown an aptitude and interest in art, Professor of Mathematics William Church had inspired him like no other instructor. The subject was easy for him, "so easy . . . as to come almost by intuition." Not so, the other subjects. An old classmate, Rufe Ingalls, recalled that he was careless and lazy, spending little time in study and making no effort to memorize those subjects requiring it. He had no time for the classics or his French homework and "rarely read over a lesson a second time." Romantic novels were more to his liking. Being shy he developed no early friendships. Ofttimes lonesome and sometimes homesick, he found comfort in his room devouring novels.

17

PANORAMIC V[...]

SIGHT-SEEING IN NEW YORK—On his way to West Point, Ulysses stopped off at Pittsburg and Philadelphia, his last stop being New York. This view in 1840 by Robert Havell was something to write home about. Courtesy Prints Division, New York Public Library.

Autumn brought some solace in another respect. With more attention given to studies there was less emphasis on hazing. And there was time for girls, but they were not for Sam. Military balls were frequent but Sam did not dance and had no wish to learn.

He still maintained a secret desire to leave the Academy. Later he was to write, "A military life had no charms for me, and I had not the slightest idea of staying in the Army even if I should be graduated, which I did not expect."

About this time a bill appeared before Congress calling for the abolishment of the Academy. Claiming that the school was inefficient and wasting the taxpayer's money, the sponsors of the bill pointed it out as a breeding ground for snobbery. Reading the reports of the debate with great interest, Sam "was selfish enough to favor the bill." Though it never passed, a year later, he recalled, "although time hung drearily with me, I would have been sorry to have seen it succeed."

There was a possible consolation for all this. Doing well with his mathematics, now that his six months probationary period was over, it was his desire to graduate and obtain the position of assistant professor of mathematics at the Academy. Later, perhaps, he might obtain a professorship at some college.

In a letter to a cousin in Bethel during that September, he wrote how much he loved the Academy, and "it seems as though I could live her forever, if my friends would come too." He had no prejudices against any instructor nor did he have any disagreeable episode with any of his classmates. Rufe Ingalls had been a close friend during this plebe year even though he had inveigled Sam into a forbidden trip to Benny Havens'. The renowned tavern was off limits.

With the passing of the plebe year and its limitations, Sam was free to make friendships in the upper classes. Pete Longstreet and Lafayette McLaws, both southerners, and Calvin Benjamin from Indiana, all from the Junior class, struck a common bond. And then there was Alfred Sully in the senior class for whom he developed a strong attachment.

The use of tobacco in any form was not permitted, a regulation that stimulated the chewing habit because of the ease with which the habit could be hidden. Sam tried to smoke, got sick, gave it up. It is not recorded whether he took to chewing tobacco. He did drink with the boys on occasion but swore off with some of the others in an attempt to remove the temptation from a classmate who had little willpower.

He may not have been the finest student in the

NEW YORK.

Academy though he was in the top section of mathematics. His fencing was mediocre, his dancing intolerable. But in horsemanship he had no match. Had it counted toward class standing he would have graduated much nearer the top.

Riding had been added to the curriculum in 1839, the first instructor being James McAuley, who held this post until six months before the Class of '43 graduated. Sergeant Henry R. Herschberger followed him as riding master.

Few of the horses were good. One of the intractable ones was a powerful sorrel called York. It was young Grant who thought he could be ridden and proved it. York's habit of rearing and tumbling over backwards confused most riders, but not Grant. Even McAuley couldn't handle York. Sam stuck to him like a burr, breaking him of the rearing by tapping him between the ears with a pistol butt. Then, patiently, he taught him better manners. From then on York was his horse. As he used to say: "If I can mount a horse I can ride him."

General James B. Fry and others have described Cadet Grant's leap to Academy fame. In June of 1843, in a riding hall full of spectators, and following demonstrations in horsemanship, he was ordered to display his jumping ability over the high hurdle. On York he galloped the length of the hall, clearing the bar "as if man and beast had been welded together." Whether it was five feet six inches or

more than six feet, no one is certain. His high jump record stood for over 25 years.

Meanwhile Jesse's business was growing. The need for shoes and harness in the rapidly developing midwest offered vast opportunity to a man with his ambition. He had visited Galena, Illinois, a famous lead-mining center on the Fevre River three miles from the Mississippi River, and seen the fortunes being made in lead, commission houses and the shipping trade. He had seen too the steamer loads of buffalo skins arriving from the northwest, and the farmers bringing in cowhides to the Mississippi Valley town. Here was opportunity.

About 1840 he sold his Georgetown tannery and formed a partnership with E. A. Collins, who owned a tannery 12 miles away in Bethel, Clermont County. He moved to Bethel to take over the tannery and expand it, while Collins opened a leather-goods store in their names. When Jesse's second son, Samuel Simpson, became 18 (1843) he would spend part of his time in the Galena store. Jesse would stay in Bethel turning out tanned hides in his large tannery for the wholesale trade.

At the end of his first two years, Sam's class received the customary ten-week furlough that extended from the middle of June following examinations until August 28th. He left for home number 24 in a class of 53, standing well in the middle, about in the same position he would graduate.

VIEW OF WEST POINT.

WEST POINT—From a drawing by Seth Eastman. Courtesy United States Military Academy.

GENERAL-IN-CHIEF WINFIELD SCOTT—Grant first saw him during the first year encampment at West Point. He thought him "the finest specimen of manhood my eyes had ever beheld, and the most to be envied." At the time Scott was a large man, very commanding in appearance, and wore a very showy uniform. Courtesy Library of Congress.

MARTIN VAN BUREN—When President Van Buren visited West Point in the summer of 1841 he did not impress Sam with the awe General Scott had inspired. Courtesy Library of Congress.

VIEW OF WEST POINT,
UNITED STATES MILITARY ACADEMY.

WEST POINT IN GRANT'S DAY—View from Fort Putnam painted by Robert Havell, 1848. Courtesy United States Military Academy.

Going home for the first time was a happy occasion. His father had purchased a fine bay colt for him that had not been broken to harness. He enjoyed the colt as he enjoyed the round of visits to his relatives and old friends. It was a peaceful, restful summer—no routine—no drums to govern the tempo of his every move.

When the furlough ended he returned to the Academy to find the commandant had appointed him a sergeant, the last of 18 in the new junior class. The promotion was more than he could bear for he was not much of a sergeant, and in a matter of time he was relieved of the awful responsibility. Once back in the ranks, he remained a private until his graduation.

As graduation time neared he realized he had not been the best student. He had absorbed the useful substance from the various courses without cluttering his mind with the detail that is necessary to obtain high marks. And though he did not know it then, he was able to size up his classmates so as to take advantage of their weaknesses and habits of thinking 20 years later.

SECOND LIEUTENANTS U. S. GRANT AND ALEXANDER HAYS—Taken at camp Salubrity, Louisiana in 1845. At the left is Grant's racing horse **Dandy** behind him, and on the right is Hays' pony **Sunshine**. Hays and Grant had been fellow cadets at West Point. Both served in the same regiment during the war with Mexico. Hays was killed at the battle of the Wilderness leading his troops. Courtesy United States Military Academy Archives.

A PAINTING BY CADET U. S. GRANT—Entitled "Indians Bargaining," was made by him in 1841. Courtesy West Point Museum Collections.

Men like "Pete" Longstreet, "Bill" Sherman, George Thomas, "Rosey" Rosecrans, Rufe Ingalls, Simon Buckner, Reynolds, McClellan, Hardie, Augur, Coppee, Fry and his last roommate, Fred Dent, were but a few of those who would make names for themselves.

In years to come he would think of West Point as the best school in the world for discipline where "a boy to go through four years . . . must have the essential elements of a strong, manly character," or he would fail. His experience there had not been the happiest portion of his life. If anything his stay had been the most trying days in his life, which he could not recall with pleasure.

In recording a choice of the branch of service preferred at graduation time, Sam requested the cavalry, or dragoons, as the only such regiment in the army was called then. His second choice was the Fourth Infantry, and to that he was assigned. He had been 16th in engineering, 25th in artillery tactics, 28th in ethics, 156th on the conduct roll of a corps of 233, with 66 demerits for this fourth year totaling 290 for the four years. Not high, not low, but right in the middle of the plank he rode, graduating number 21 in a class of 39, a class that had started with 76 four years before. His grades had been tolerable. Certainly no George B. McClellan or Douglas MacArthur.

ARTILLERY PRACTICE AT WEST POINT—Painting by George Catlin. Courtesy West Point Museum Collections.

Chapter Three

Tempered by War

Reluctant was the word for Ulysses. He had been adverse to the acceptance of an appointment to West Point but his father had thought otherwise. He had conformed to, but had not absorbed fully, the teachings of the Academy. He had hopes of becoming an instructor of mathematics rather than a soldier, a hope that still prevailed, for Professor of Mathematics William Church had assured him he would receive a call to fill a faculty position as soon as a vacancy occurred. For once in his life he became a student, reviewing his West Point course in mathematics "with regularity, if not persistency."

Following graduation, and up until it was necessary to go to Jefferson Barracks, he had spent a leisurely vacation with his parents at Bethel, having arrived there with a bad cough contracted some six months earlier. Called "Tyler's Grip," it had cut his weight to 117 pounds. On entering the Academy four years prior, he had weighed the same though he had been six inches shorter. His family was alarmed since tuberculosis was prevalent on his father's side, two of Jesse's brothers having died of it. During the Civil War Ulysses' brother Samuel and sister Clara died of it.

His father had sold the tannery and turned to farming. Ulysses' welcome arrival was occasion for a new saddle horse for his own use besides a horse and buggy. Though he did not feel at his best on arrival, three months of family home nursing and ministration almost rid him of his persistent cough and weight loss.

Arriving at Jefferson Barracks, St. Louis, on the 20th of September to join the Fourth United States Infantry, Ulysses spent the first few months of spare time at his studies. There at the largest military post in the country, he found eight companies of the Fourth Infantry and eight companies of the Third Infantry. Joining the Fourth Infantry as a brevet second lieutenant, he discovered among its officers James Longstreet, who had graduated in 1842, being number 60 in a class of 62. Longstreet was related to his former roommate, Fred Dent, whose parents lived but five miles west of the post.

Since Fred Dent had been ordered to report to a post farther west, he was unable to introduce his roommate to his family. Ulysses, having taken his favorite saddle horse with him from Ohio, spent part of his time in riding. One day he rode out the Gravois Road about a mile past the intersection with the Barracks Road, to the Dent estate. The white house on it was called White Haven. As he approached the turnstile that headed the path leading to

PRESIDENT JOHN TYLER—Tyler was in full accord with the move to annex Texas. From a Daguerreotype. Courtesy Library of Congress.

the house, a white child of about six, and four pickaninnies, came up to him. After repeatedly asking the white girl if Mr. Dent lived there, he finally received an affirmative answer. This was Fred's baby sister Emma.

After he informed the slave at the door that he was Fred's roommate, a short, slender, grey-eyed woman of middle age and a girl of 15 greeted him. These were Fred's mother and his sister Ellen. He was introduced to Fred's father, "Colonel" Frederick Dent, a St. Louis merchant.

The Colonel was a white-haired man of 56, medium height, smooth-shaven; a man who was hot-tempered, quarrelsome and opinionated. Sitting on his front porch rocking chair and smoking a long pipe, he enjoyed discussing politics with the young lieutenant. Being a Jacksonian Democrat, he viewed all Whigs and Abolitionists with hostility. In contrast Ulysses spoke quietly and in even tones, using common sense and sound logic in presenting his views. Mrs. Dent enjoyed Ulysses' argumentation and was one of the first to predict a great future for him.

Though young Grant was a farmer at heart and loved the land, his twice weekly visits to the Dent plantation were the natural result of his loneliness being erased by the Dent congeniality. The large family had made him feel as one of them. The oldest son, John, now 24, was home, along with Louis, age 20, Ellen, nicknamed "Nellie," 16, and Emma, 6. Brothers George, 22, and Frederick, 23, and sister Julia, 17, were away. George

was married and Julia was spending the winter with kinfolks in St. Louis, the O'Fallons, attending Professor Moreau's school and adding to her knowledge of music, ballroom etiquette, French and poetry.

Julia heard much of the young lieutenant in her letters from home. He, in turn, heard much of her at the Dent hearth. When they first met in February of 1844, they were not strangers. With him it was love at first sight.

Julia was a well-formed girl barely five feet high, with tiny hands and feet. Her flawless skin, warm complexion, dark, thick glossy hair drawn back tightly to her head, made a young man look twice. She played and sang well, and was an excellent dancer and horsewoman. Though she was the plainest looking of the Dent girls, she was the most gracious and charming to meet.

Ulysses was five feet eight inches tall, slender of figure, with regular features. He had a straight, stubborn mouth, a firm chin, plump, rosy cheeks set in a porcelain complexion that was easy to flush, clear, blue eyes and a heavy head of fine, wavy brown hair. He did not dance nor was he socially inclined. A common ground was their love of riding, an interest that drew them together often.

Though Julia and Ulysses had grown up in contrasting backgrounds, both had prudent, modest mothers and stubborn, opinionated fathers. With a background of military and pioneer ancestry, each could claim a vigorous childhood. Inevitably they became constant companions. Whether at the gar-

BATTLE OF PALO ALTO, MEXICO—On May 8, 1846, Grant was under fire for the first time. General Zachary Taylor led and won it. Courtesy National Archives.

BRIGADIER GENERAL TO PRESIDENT—Franklin Pierce, a veteran of the war with Mexico, became President by winning as a Democrat over General Scott in November of 1853. Courtesy Library of Congress.

rison dances where he watched her dance to music his tone-deaf ear could not appreciate or in the saddle riding the valley land on sunny spring days, he was always near her. He did not know if it was love that made him want to be with her constantly for he was a phlegmatic, slow-burning type.

During this time Congress was discussing the annexation of Texas, with President Tyler making vigorous efforts to effect it. Over 100 miles north and somewhat parallel to the Rio Grande River is the Nueces River, both running into the Gulf of Mexico. The Texans claimed as their territory the land extending to the Rio Grande. The Mexicans declared their northern border to be the Nueces. The almost worthless piece of land between the two rivers finally was occupied by American troops.

Preparatory to this occupation, the Third Infantry was ordered to Fort Jesup, Louisiana, leaving Jefferson Barracks about the first of May, 1844. At this same time Grant received a 20 day leave to visit his parents. Just after he had left, the Fourth Infantry also received orders to proceed to Fort Jesup. Returning to Jefferson Barracks, he received orders to join his command from Lieutenant Richard Ewell, who graciously granted

a few days' additional leave. He had little time to do what he knew he must do. Proceeding on horseback to the Dents, he met Julia. As he related: "Before separating it was definitely understood that at a convenient time we would join our fortunes . . ." This agreement was fulfilled four years later.

The Third Infantry had been stationed at the Fort Jesup military reservation 20 miles southwest of Natchitoches, midway between the Sabine and Red Rivers. Grant joined his regiment at Camp Salubrity three miles north of Natchitoches. It was here he spent the winter with the "Army of Observation," an army that appeared to him with his pacifistic nature as one that had been placed on the border of Texas for the express purpose of goading Mexico into an unjust war. The life in the open air that winter had one salutary effect—he lost the last trace of his nagging cough. Here, as at Jefferson Barracks, he spent a goodly share of his free time riding around the countryside on his favorite saddle horse.

Late in the spring of '45 he obtained a leave that permitted him to visit the Dents and obtain the parental consent for Julia's hand. Resentfully Colonel Dent yielded for the appeal had the firm support of both his wife and his son Fred.

THE STORMING OF MONTEREY, MEXICO—On September 23, 1846, Grant volunteered to carry a message for General Garland, doing so under heavy fire. Courtesy National Archives.

GENERAL D. ANTONIO LOPEZ DE SANTA-ANNA.

PRESIDENT OF THE REPUBLIC OF MEXICO.

By **A. Hoffy**, from an original likeness taken from life at **Vera-Cruz**.

The above is a correct likeness from our personal observation

E. W. Moore

Com. late Texas Navy.

Alex. C. Blount

Published July 1847, by **A. HOFFY**, N°. 20, South Third S.' near Chesnut, Philad.ª

& by **JOHNSON & BROCKETT**, N°. 28, South Seventh S.'bet. Chesnut & Walnut.

GENERAL ANTONIO LOPEZ DE SANTA ANNA — President Polk permitted Santa Anna to slip back into Mexico, seize the Government and make peace with the United States. Instead he preached war. Repeatedly he was defeated by U. S. Forces, finally going into hiding. Engraving by A. Hoffy. Courtesy Library of Congress.

In March of 1845 a joint resolution of both houses of Congress decreed the annexation of Texas. President Tyler lost no time in accomplishing this by ordering an "Army of Occupation" to take over. Though Grant was not in favor of this attempt to provoke war with Mexico, he knew his duty and accepted it without question.

Stopping first at New Orleans to obtain supplies, the Third and Fourth Regiments sailed from there in the middle of July when President Polk found that his diplomatic endeavors with Mexico had failed. He ordered the commanding officer, General Zachary Taylor, to continue on to the Nueces with his troops. Landing at Corpus Christi, they made a campsite at the mouth of the river. Though Texas had claimed this strip of land it previously had received permission to colonize from the Mexican government, Grant noted there were no Texans settled on it.

That December Sam received notice that, effective September 30th last, his rank was that of a full second lieutenant. Only five of his 38 classmates had received this promotion, five others receiving it with him.

During the winter the officers organized an amateur theatrical group in which Sam was a flop in the female role of Desdemona. Equally unsuccessful was his part in a wild turkey hunt. On the one occasion he went he became so interested in watching the flight of the birds he forgot to take the shotgun off his shoulder. His hunting companion, Calvin Benjamin, shot as many as he could carry back. Though it was plentiful, Sam would not eat fowl of any kind and would only sample venison if it was very well done.

He purchased a few horses at three dollars apiece, losing them in one fell swoop when they ran away together. This resulted in General Taylor's adjutant getting a laugh with: "Yes, I heard Grant lost five or six dollars worth of horses the other day."

Grant's favorite mount had cost 12 dollars. The temperamental stallion had been feared and refused by all of the officers, but Sam believed he could break it if it did not break his neck first. The untamed animal was blindfolded and equipped with a heavy bit and a huge Spanish saddle. Once Sam had mounted, the horse trembled momentarily, then began a succession of bucking, fish-tailing and twisting gyrations. This continued for some time—to the delight of the growing crowd of

soldiers—until Grant felt the animal falter. Driving in his spurs caused the animal to break into a dead gallop for the plains, disappearing with Grant in the distance. It was more than three hours before they returned, a docile stallion carrying a victorious master. According to Pete Longstreet the ride was a subject of discussion in every camp in the country.

It was apparent that Mexico could not be provoked into a war. As Grant had said: "We were sent to provoke a fight, but it was essential that Mexico should commence it." Accordingly Taylor was given orders to move his troops to the Rio Grande River near Matamoras.

Leaving a thousand men to hold Corpus Christi, the troops proceeded over the 150 mile strip with few incidents. They did not sight the Mexican army until within a dozen miles of Metamoras. Captain McCall estimated the enemy at 6,000 of which 1,200 were cavalrymen—and 10 cannon. The American force of 3,000 looked small indeed.

This first engagement occurred near Palo Alto on the morning of May 8th. It was principally an artillery duel in which Taylor had the advantage. The Mexicans opened fire with their brass six-pounders throwing solid shot. General Taylor

GENERAL SCOTT LANDING AT VERA CRUZ—Scott's forces landed on the beaches near Vera Cruz, March 9, 1847, without a shot being fired at them. Courtesy National Archives.

HOUSE TO HOUSE FIGHTING—Much of the Mexican campaign required street fighting. This painting by Eugene Chaperon shows the dress and equipment of the U. S. officers and men. Courtesy National Archives.

returned the fire with four 12-pounders throwing shells and two 18-pounders loaded with canister. The effect of the musketry was minimal because both sides used flint and ball with a range much shorter and less effective than the cannon. The Americans advanced under the fire of their cannon, the battle of Palo Alto ending once they occupied the ground held by the Mexicans who had retreated a few miles south to Resaca de la Palma. Nine Americans had been killed and 47 wounded.

On the following morning Taylor's army advanced through an almost impenetrable chaparral following trails that could easily be ambushed. Resistance was first met and quickly overcome at a series of ponds. There being no further resistance, the army camped on ground now occupied by the city of Brownsville, named in honor of Major Jacob Brown, commander of the Seventh Infantry who had been killed in the battle.

Leaving a small garrison at Matamoras on August 19th—for they had learned they were now an "Army of Invasion" because of the acts of Mexico—they proceeded toward Monterey. Up to this time the army consisted entirely of regulars. Now it was reinforced with one-year volunteers. One of them from Ohio was Thomas L. Hamer, a brigadier general, who had appointed Grant to West Point.

Detailed as the regimental quartermaster and commissary, Grant had his difficulties with the Fourth Infantry's wagons and pack train. Horses proved inadequate in the mountainous country and had to be replaced with pack mules. Though Grant never had used profanity in his life, the difficulties encountered by those in charge of the animals made him excuse those who found it expedient to use it.

With 6,500 men General Taylor began his attack on Monterey September 21, 1846. Monterey was a city of nearly 20,000 defended by General Pedro de Ampudia and an army of 10,000 officers and men. Taylor's lieutenants, Generals W. O. Butler, David E. Twiggs and especially William J. Worth, rendered unusual service in the three days of sharp fighting that ended in American victory.

At one point in the battle within the city, Colonel John Garland's ten companies of men could neither advance nor retreat, finally running out of ammunition. After a call for a volunteer to reach General Twiggs for ammunition and reinforcements, Lieutenant Grant offered to go. Riding on the side of his horse Indian style, he dashed full speed down a side street, bullets flying at him from every crossing. At one point his horse took a four-foot wall in an easy leap, soon reaching Twiggs. Though there was a great deal of discussion about his ride, his name did not appear in the reports. Young officers rarely were mentioned, brevets coming more easily to the higher ranking officers.

Following the surrender on September 24th, Grant noted: "The prisoners were paroled and permitted to take their horses with them . . . . I question whether the great majority of the Mexican people did not regret our departure that midwinter as much as they regretted our coming. Property and person were thoroughly protected, and a market was afforded for all products of the country such as the people had never enjoyed before."

During the occupation of Monterey, Colonel Dent had financial difficulties as the result of a lawsuit. Julia magnanimously offered to release Ulysses but, needless to say, the offer was refused. Grant's one other concern had been the sudden illness of his friend and patron Tom Hamer that had ended in his death just before the battle of Monterey. He felt the loss keenly as he knew his father Jesse would.

The victories at Matamoras and Monterey made General Taylor a national hero and a presidential possibility. President Polk, realizing that the popular Taylor was being promoted as a Whig candidate to oppose him in the next election, decided to send the general-in-chief, Winfield Scott, into the field. Scott was a Whig with known presidential aspirations. Polk reasoned that Scott would cut into Taylor's popularity and lessen his chance of political success. The Polk administration then attempted to replace Scott and otherwise harass him into making a false move.

On February 22, 23 and 24, 1847, General Taylor's volunteer army fought and won against great odds at Buena Vista, the result of which the already popular Taylor was nominated for the Presidency by the Whig party.

Grant worshiped Zachary Taylor for here was a kind of officer he had never seen before. At West Point his superior officers had been spotless, precise and impeccably dressed. "Old Rough and Ready" Taylor was quick of tongue and large of heart. Grant had seen him in his uniform but once—the rest of the time he wore muddy boots, a straw hat and plain clothes without insignia. A natural leader of men, he was uneducated, eccentric, yet popular with his soldiers. And most important, he always won his battles. If Grant worshiped him so did the American voters—they elected him President in 1848.

"Old Fuss and Feathers" Scott landed his 12,000 troops on the sandy beaches of Vera Cruz, then surrounded the city and began a siege. After five

BLOWING UP THE FOUNDRY AT MOLINO DEL REY—Grant participated in this battle of September 8th. Gen. Worth led the victorious American army. Courtesy National Archives.

31

days of artillery bombardment, and as he was about to open an assault, the city capitulated. Ten days later Scott was on his way to Mexico City. On the third day of this leg of the campaign he reached the foot of snow clad mountains, one of the summits of which was Cerro Gordo. General Santa Anna had retreated to this point and entrenched his 12,000 men after his defeat by Taylor at Buena Vista.

Finding the mountain passes commanded by Mexican cannon, Scott assigned an engineer, Captain Robert E. Lee, to the task of finding a solution. There followed several days of reconnaissance and preparation, during which Twigg's men dragged howitzers up the precipitous peak. The Mexicans then were flanked by American guns commanding every position but the crest. At dawn of April 18th a heavy fire drove the astounded Mexicans from their positions and resulted in their capitulation. With 3,000 prisoners, 5,000 muskets and 43 cannon taken from the enemy, Scott moved on to Puebla, reaching there May 15th. In a 60 day campaign he had captured 60,000 prisoners, 700 cannon and several important cities.

After three months of rest for his weary troops, many of whom were ill with dysentery, Scott resumed the march toward the capital. With a force of 11,000 opposed by double this number, the great test was yet to come. Following skirmishes at San Augustin, a hand-to-hand battle at Contreras that ended in victory and yet another victory at Churubusco, Scott spent several weeks unsuccessfully attempting to negotiate a peace with Santa Anna.

By September 7th Scott discovered that Santa Anna was using the armistice only as a means of recuperation for his army. Breaking off the negotiations, Scott ordered Worth to begin an immediate assault upon the outer defenses of Mexico City. This he did at daylight of the next day. The low stone buildings they were attacking, called Molino del Rey (Mill of the King), were at the right and the foot of Chapultepec (Hill of the Grasshoppers). They were heavily defended. Worth's forces were repulsed there several times because he had ordered the attack following an inadequate preliminary artillery barrage. He finally gave the Mexicans a heavy bombardment such as he should have done in the beginning, and his charging men valiantly took the building in bloody hand-to-hand conflict. Grant, as in several of the previous engagements, managed to enter into the fray. Moving forward with the troops and finding Fred Dent wounded in the thigh from a musket ball, he lifted him to the top of a wall so the surgeons would not miss him, then rushed on. Fred accidentaly rolled off several minutes later, suffering several broken bones from which he suffered more than from the wound. By eight o'clock that morning the buildings had been taken but high above them stood mighty Chapultepec Castle. Their gain had been little; their loss had been great. With a few more such victories they would have no army.

But Scott knew the citadel above them was the key to the conquest, and take it he must. The assault was preceded by a heavy canonading which was returned from the commanding positions above. As in previous engagements, Grant was in the advance, in this instance on the San Cosme causeway near the gate to the city. The suburban approaches were being defended by barricades and riflemen on housetops, and the San Cosme gate was defended by several cannon that prevented any advance. Moving off on his own to determine the possibility of a flanking action, Grant discovered a church whose broad belfry commanded a view of the entrance to the city. With a dozen volunteers he forced his way in, then had his men carry a disassembled howitzer to the belfry where it was used to effectively shell and dislodge the enemy.

Worth, observing the effects of this act of resourcefulness and common sense, called Grant to him and offered his congratulations. Three commanders referred to him in their official reports. It was Colonel Garland who reported: "I must not omit to call attention to Lieutenant Grant, who acquitted himself most nobly upon several occasions under my observation." He added: "A howitzer which, under the direction of Lieutenant Grant, quartermaster of the Fourth Infantry, and Lieutenant Lendrum of the Third Artillery, annoyed the enemy considerably."

With the fall of the Chapultepec, long used as the Mexican military academy, the gates of the city were breached. The better part of a week was taken to mop up and overcome the armed resistance within it. As the hostilities drew to a close, Grant discovered that his close friend, Calvin Benjamin, had been killed in a valorous action at the Belen Gate. Quietly he bore his grief though the death of Tom Hamer still was on his mind.

The only consolation was the knowledge that he just had been made a first lieutenant.

During the eight months in Mexico City with the army of occupation, much of Grant's time as regimental quartermaster was spent in procuring supplies. Renting a bakery and obtaining a contract to bake bread for the chief of commissary, he made more money for the regimental fund than he received as pay for the entire war.

Leisure time was spent in learning Spanish, mountain climbing and horse racing. On one occasion he visited a bullfight which he did not see to the finish, the sight being revolting to him. He said he could not see "how human beings could enjoy the sufferings of beasts, and often of men, as they seemed to do on these occasions." When, as President, bullfights were given in his honor on his visits to Mexico, he would tactfully avoid them.

Drinking was a custom in Scott's army and those who did not were considered strange indeed. Liquor was supplied at the officers' mess; there was no excuse to be dry. Many who were lonely found solace in its use, Grant not excepted.

The peace commissioners resolved their differences during this period and on February 2, 1848,

ASSAULT ON CHAPULTEPEC—U. S. infantry climb Grasshopper Hill to reach the castle. Courtesy National Archives.

BATTLE OF CHAPULTEPEC, MEXICO CITY—The castle was stormed on September 13th. Within two days the city had capitulated. Courtesy National Archives.

signed the Treaty of Guadalupe Hidalgo which designated the Rio Grande River as a boundary between the two countries, ceding Texas, New Mexico and Upper California to the United States for the sum of 15 million dollars.

The Mexican War had lasted 26 months, costing $160,000,000, with losses averaging 1,000 men a month. In contrast, the Civil War lasted 48 months, costing $3,400,000,000 ($2-1/2 million a day), with losses averaging 700 men a day.

In later life Grant wrote: "My experience in the Mexican War was of great advantage to me afterward. Besides the many practical lessons it taught, the war brought nearly all the officers of the regular army together as to make them personally acquainted. . . . I had been at West Point at about the right time to meet most of the graduates who were of suitable age at the breaking out of the rebellion to be trusted with large commands. . . . These classes embraced more than 50 officers who afterward became generals on one side or other in the rebellion, many of them holding high commands. . . . My appreciation of my enemies was certainly affected by this knowledge."

As Grant stated, there were many lessons learned in the Mexican War: the simplicity of Taylor's army regulations in comparison with Scott's severe discipline, Scott's successful operations with gunboats and artillery at Vera Cruz, the paroling of armies instead of imprisonment to put them in a better frame of mind for peace, cutting loose from a base of supplies was not logistically dangerous, a night march was a valuable tool, front line troops will follow anyone who will lead, entrenchments were to be distrusted, a frontal attack was a speedy road to victory, attacks on fortifications could be successful with small odds of 2 to 1 or 3 to 1, charging uphill against batteries was not risky, and most important—make the best of things.

In July of 1848 the Fourth Infantry embarked at Vera Cruz for Pascagoula, Mississippi, to camp for the summer. Grant obtained a four month leave during which he proceeded to St. Louis, marrying Julia Dent in her home on August 22, 1848. After visiting the Grants at Bethel and the Simpsons at Bantam, the newlyweds headed for Detroit to join his regiment, arriving there November 17th. The newly established Detroit Barracks had no quartermaster's post available so he was ordered on to Madison Barracks in Sacketts Harbor, New York.

34

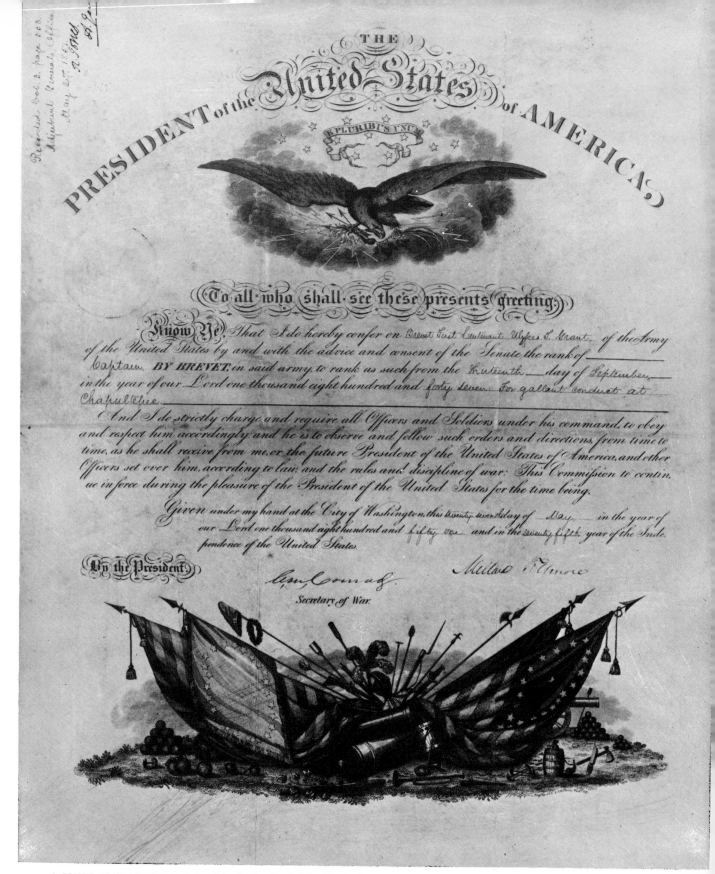

A BREVET AT CHAPULTEPEC—Going into the battle of Palo Alto in May, 1846, as a second lieutenant, Grant had obtained a brevet rank of the first lieutenant, then captain, but remained a second lieutenant when he entered Mexico City 16 months later. Courtesy Smithsonian Institution.

Chapter Four

Chandler Meets His Challenge

Ulysses arrived at Sacketts Harbor under protest. As quartermaster of the Fourth Infantry stationed at Detroit, he believed his place to be with his regiment. His Madison Barracks commander, Major Francis Lee, agreed with him by placing the grievance before General Scott. Scott too agreed, sending him back to Detroit. The order came too late, ice having closed navigation on the Great Lakes, so it was spring before they made their move.

Arriving in Detroit in March and taking temporary quarters at the National Hotel, Julia and Ulysses observed a frontier post that had grown to a city of 20,000. Soon after, they moved into a small frame home at 253 East Fort Street, the rent being $250 a year. The house stood between Russell and Rivard Streets not far from the barracks, which extended some five blocks from Catherine Street to the Gratiot Road and from Rivard to Russell. The Detroit Barracks, which were abandoned in June, 1851, had buildings of wood, and were surrounded by a board fence.

Though his duties as quartermaster held little interest for him, there was little actual work involved. He had learned much from this assignment during the Mexican campaign where procurement and logistics had been stimulating problems; here it was a matter of boring and repetitive paper work. This was relieved by the assignment to him of a clerk, Friend Palmer, who assumed most of the responsibility and all of the paper work.

These were happy days for Ulysses, even though they were days of inaction. Relieved from the monotony of his military office routine by an efficient clerk, he took the newlywed's delight in a new wife and a home of his own. Away from home his thoughts turned to horses. Jim Cicotte, a prosperous Detroit Democrat, had a small, black trotting mare that took Grant's fancy. Buying it for $250, he wagered $50 his new "French pony" "could go with two men in the buggy, a mile inside of three minutes." In 1849 Detroit was small enough for the story to spread rapidly around town. The French inhabitants took a personal interest in this event for one principal was the French mare and the other Cicotte's father who had been selected by Grant to do the driving.

Starting on Grand River Avenue at about Trumbull Boulevard, the little mare made the mile easily inside the three minute limit. The Frenchmen went wild and even Grant showed some emotion. After caressing his horse and seeing her well cared for, he took his friends to the old *Shades* on Shelby Street, between Larned and Jefferson Avenue. The celebrants were not permitted to leave until refreshed at least a dozen times.

As the winter of 1850 passed the Grants stopped attending the various functions; Julia was with child. With the baby expected around the first of June, Julia left in the spring for her home in St. Louis. Ulysses moved in with their good friends, Captain and Mrs. John Gore, who lived on Jefferson Avenue at the corner of Russell Street. The boy Julia gave him was born May 30, 1850, and promptly was named Frederick Dent Grant.

Though reading little, Grant smoked a pipe constantly and played cards a great deal. In a group of close friends and associates, he was most agreeable and talkative; if there were strangers present, he had little to say. His speech became animated when discussing the Mexican War and he would describe battle scenes vividly with infinite detail.

On Jefferson Street two doors below Woodward was the sutler's store, common meeting place and source of news. The officers would meet there most every day. In the back room was a barrel of whisky and a tin cup, generously supplied by the sutler. Each visitor helped himself, Grant among them. Drinking was a part of Detroit's social etiquette and was expected of everyone.

Julia soon returned to Detroit, arriving there by July. Summer and fall passed languidly and uneventfully, for the newborn occupied the full attention of the proud parents. There was time, however, to race the Cicotte mare.

Detroit's "Mr. Big" in 1851 was Zachariah Chandler. After amassing a fortune in merchandising drygoods and investing wisely in real estate, he turned his great energy to politics. Detroit, then in the throes of a boom, had a population of 25,000. The Mayor was paid no salary; he received one

GRANT ACQUIRES A FATHER-IN-LAW—Colonel Frederick Dent was a cantankerous Jacksonian Democrat who had little desire for a military son-in-law but was outmaneuvered by his wife and daughter Julia. A loving father, he was less so with those who crossed him outside his family. Though having little faith in Ulysses he did assist him on a few occasions and was quick to collect payment in the way of extended visits to the White House when it housed a Grant. Courtesy Library of Congress.

dollar for each case tried in the Mayor's Court. The thought of being the mayor appealed to Chandler. Crude, cunning, ruthless, yet honest, he decided to make his first run for office in this Democratic stronghold as a Whig.

Then as now the city required homeowners to clear ice and snow off sidewalks. It seems that various officers of the post had been slipping on the neglected sidewalks in front of Chandler's Jefferson Avenue residence. One night while returning home from headquarters, Grant slipped and sprained an ankle in front of Chandler's. His sworn complaint stated:

"that on or about the 10th day of January, 1851, and for 25 days previous thereto, within the City of Detroit, Zachariah Chandler did

THE DENT HOME—WHITE HAVEN—It was here that Ulysses met Julia. Behind this house stood the barns, stables and slave quarters. Courtesy St. Louis Public Library.

WHERE GRANT GOT MARRIED—It was in this corner house that Ulysses married Julia Dent on August 22, 1848. The winter home of his father-in-law Colonel Frederick Dent, it stood on the northeast corner of Fourth and Cerre Streets in St. Louis. Courtesy Missouri Historical Society.

neglect to keep his sidewalk clear and free from snow and ice on Jefferson Avenue, in front of his house occupied by him . . ."

Chandler insisted upon a jury and conducted his own case. Denouncing Grant, Gore and Major Sibley as idle loafers living on the community, he said: "If you soldiers would keep sober, perhaps you would not fall on people's pavements and hurt your legs."

Chandler lost his case although the jury was sympathetic to him as a civilian. They assessed a fine of six cents and court costs which ran less than eight dollars. Fifteen years later the litigants would laugh at the incident when Grant, as General of the Armies, was Chandler's house guest in Detroit.

That spring the War Department abandoned the Detroit Barracks, sending Grant and the Fourth Infantary to Sacketts Harbor, New York. This town of 1,000 was quite a contrast to the exciting post they had just left. Arriving in June, they soon settled down to the slower pace of Madison Barracks. Ulysses attended the weekly meetings of the Independent Order of Odd Fellows though he never became an officer. Both he and Julia attended the Sacketts Harbor Presbyterian Church. Then Ulysses decided to give up drinking by joining the local Rising Sun chapter of the Sons of Temperance. Grant held a succession of offices in the lodge, abstaining from the use of alcoholic beverages in any form during his residence there.

Restless and energetic, he had to be busy. Family, lodges, church, military affairs—all provided an

DETROIT IN 1852—A view of Detroit from the Michigan Central Railroad Wheat Depot. Detroit River and Canadian shores on the right. Drawn and lithographed by R. Burger. Courtesy Detroit Historical Museum.

outlet. When the decrease of activity in the winter there was time for horse racing on the ice. On one such occasion, when two of his acquaintances, Phillips and DeWolf, were running a horse, the animal became excited at the shouting of the watching crowd. When the horse began to run away, Phillips jumped out of the cutter with the reins in his hands. With great risk DeWolf recovered the reins and brought the horse under control. Ulysses hotly charged Phillips with being a coward and ordered him never to speak to him again for having deserted his friend.

With the arrival of spring came orders for the regiment that would take it to the west coast. Julia had been pregnant all of that winter. It was decided that she and little Fred would go to Bethel and live with Hannah and Jesse. They would be sent for when the two children were old enough to travel—perhaps in a year.

Jesse still continued on a timetable. Then 57, his final milestone was to be a planned retirement at age 60. With tanneries in Bethel and Portsmouth, Ohio, leathergoods stores in Galena, Illinois, LaCrosse, Wisconsin, and a small one in Iowa, and several sons active in his business ventures, he was worth well over $100,000. At this time, Jesse was mayor of Bethel, having been so since its incorporation that year.

Ulysses knew his family would be welcome, and so they were. Parting on June 15th, Julia and little Fred left for Bethel, Ulysses for Governor's Island. Little did they know their separation would be for two long, lonely years.

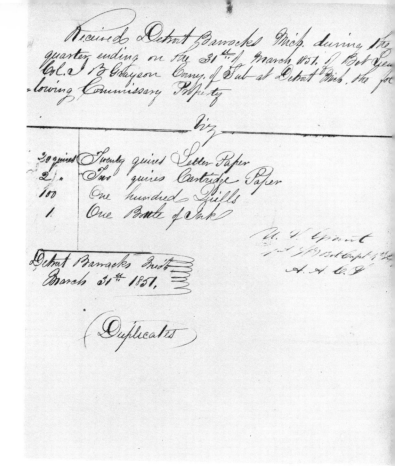

DETROIT BARRACKS CORRESPONDENCE—March 31, 1851. Courtesy Chicago Historical Society.

GRANT'S DETROIT RESIDENCE—Located at 253 East Fort Street, and now permanently at the Michigan State Fair Grounds, it was occupied by the Grants during 1849-1850. Courtesy Burton Historical Collections, Detroit Public Library.

GRANT GOES TO COURT—Starting with his assignment to duty in Detroit, Grant appeared to be accident-prone. Falling on an icy pavement or under a falling horse and injuring an extremity was an act repeated quite often. Courtesy Detroit Historical Museum.

MAYOR ZACHARIAH CHANDLER—Elected in Detroit during 1851, he was paid no salary but received one dollar for each case tried in the Mayor's Court. Serving one term he then ran on the Whig ticket against the Democratic incumbent Governor from Monroe, Robert McClelland, and was defeated. Oil painting by Detroit attorney Lewis T. Ives. Courtesy Burton Historical Collection, Detroit Public Library.

SACKETS HARBOR, NEW YORK—The large three-story stone building on the left was built in 1818 as the Union Hotel. Later it became the Masonic Temple where Grant took his Masonic Degrees. Courtesy Mrs. Sydney M. Smith, Sackets Harbor, N.Y.

Sackets Harbor N.Y.
November 4th 1851

Messrs J. Carl Jr. & Co.
    Sir:
        As I have an opportunity of geting the sword belt & pompoon (articles which I wrote to you for some time since) from New York free of the Express Charges. I would beg that you do not send me those articles.

Yours &c
U. S. Grant
15th Regt. 4th Infy

not sent

SACKETS HARBOR CORRESPOND-ENCE—November 4, 1851. Courtesy Chicago Historical Society.

41

MADISON BARRACKS—Barracks serve as a background for the drill field. The officers' quarters are at right angles and to the right. Courtesy Mrs. Sydney M. Smith, Sackets Harbor, N.Y.

OFFICER'S ROW AT MADISON BARRACKS, N. Y.—These stone quarters were built in 1818. U. S. Grant as a lieutenant and brevet captain lived in the quarters to the left of the sally port. Courtesy Mrs. Sydney M. Smith, Sackets Harbor, N.Y.

Chapter Five

West Coast and Peace

A bungling War Department had booked passage on the already filled steamship side-wheeler *Ohio*. Where could they bed the Fourth Infantry's eight companies with their families, numbering over 700 persons? To Quartermaster Grant fell the task of finding room for all. It was not easy to sooth his hot-tempered commander, Lieutenant Colonel Benjamin Bonneville, but he did to some extent by building tiers of berths on deck.

Leaving Governor's Island July 5th, they arrived at Aspinwall, Panama, on the 16th, to find its streets eight to ten inches under water. They had arrived in the midst of the rainy season. At intervals, each afternoon, the rain would pour down in torrents followed by a burning, tropical sun. Grant "wondered how any person could live in Aspinwall, and . . . why anyone tried."

The Panama Railroad was completed only to the Chagres River at which point the passengers were carried by boat to Gorgona, and then 25 miles by mule to Panama City. Seven companies were sent ahead while Grant remained behind to follow with one company, and all of the soldiers with families. Added to his charge was such public property as camp and garrison equipage. The contract entered into with the steamship company provided transporation across the Isthmus as well as water transit. Reaching the point where mules were to be provided, Grant discovered the money-hungry American who was to provide them was doubling his contract fee by renting them to the California gold rush civilians who had crowded on the steamer *Ohio*. Some paid as high has $40 to ride a mule 25 miles—a mule that sold for $10 at other times.

The week's delay while waiting for transportation was fatal to many. Cholera had broken out with the result that one third of Grant's people died at Cruces or on the way out of there. Meanwhile he had dismissed the contractor and replaced him with a native who, at more than double the original contract price, helped them reach Panama City. There, two miles out in the harbor, was anchored the San Francisco boat *Golden Gate*, unable to leave because she was quarantined.

Sam was a ministering angel for countless hours beyond his duties as quartermaster. He spent over two weeks aboard a ship leased for a hospital, aiding in the nursing of the cholera victims aboard. By the time the cholera had abated, the regiment had been delayed six weeks. One sixth of all who had left with them from New York had succumbed to the epidemic. Among

SAN FRANCISCO HARBOR—1851—Courtesy Library of Congress.

the dead was his good friend Captain Gore.

The *Golden Gate* arrived at San Francisco Bay on September 15, 1852, and, after a 24 hour leave for all officers not on duty, proceeded on to Benicia Barracks for a week. From there the regiment was ordered to Columbia Barracks, Oregon Territory, near present day Portland.

A welcome sight as Grant arrived was the figure of his West Point roommate, Rufe Ingalls, standing on the bank of the Columbia River. Grant hadn't seen Rufe in seven years.

Rufe showed Sam to the house in which he would live, the "Quartermaster's Ranch." They arranged to live in it together and, to cut expenses, included Captain Thomas L. Brent. Brent had been sent to relieve Rufe as Post Quartermaster. Brent

was now a captain and was to remain there for further orders.

The Ranch became the social center for all of the officers other than the aloof and disliked Commandant Bonneville. Though this was a land of rugged beauty, it rained most of six months of the year. Rufe and Sam enjoyed their leisure hours playing cards, reminiscing and horseback riding, usually to Oregon City. The military life was routine and dull. There were no letters from home for, after leaving New York, he was cut off from his family, yet he did not complain.

After several months he received his first letter and in it was the news that his second son, Ulysses S. Grant Jr., had been born on July 22nd. A family man, Grant deeply felt the separation. There were

two solutions to his dilemma. Resignation was one. Though he was not fond of the army, it was supplying him with an income at a time he sorely needed it. If he could find a way to supplement his income so he could send for Julia and the boys, life would be bearable until something better turned up.

Discovering that San Francisco was paying outrageous prices for ice, Sam, Rufe and Lieutenant Henry D. Wallen cut 100 tons for their other partner, Captain Dall, to carry in his sailing schooner, the *Pacific Mail*. Failing winds extended the trip to six weeks. Preceded by Alaskan ships that had supplied the market, it returned empty handed. The venture proved disasterous, the speculators losing all their money.

Looking for enterprises to regain their losses, the officers decided to raise a potato crop. Vegetables were commanding the highest of prices—potatoes as much as nine dollars a bushel. Sam bought a team of decrepit horses he quickly revitalized, and used them to break up ground rented from the Hudson Bay Company. The crop resulting from their planting was enormous, and so were those of the many others who had come to a similar conclusion. Not being able to sell or give away their potatoes, other than those sold to their own mess, they were saved the task of digging them up by a benevolent overflowing Columbia River that killed most of their crop that June.

In August of the year 1853, Sam was made captain and ordered to Fort Humboldt, some 240 miles north of San Francisco. At this post there was little work or entertainment though the discipline

1 *North Bay*
2 *Contra Costa*
3 *Yerba Buena Island*
4 *California Exchange*
5 *Plaza*
6 *Leonards Warehouse*
7 *Rincon Point*

SAN FR

Published for the Histor

SAN FRANCISCO—1852—As it appeared when Grant arrived from Panama. The Gold Rush was at its peak. Courtesy California State Library.

was more inflexible and tedious. Suffering from idleness and lack of entertainment and depressed by the absence of his family, he did what many other officers did under less trying circumstances. He took to drinking. He did not drink enormous quantities, rather less than the other officers, but with his peculiar physical makeup a little liquor did the work of a great deal.

Three miles south was the lumber port of Eureka. Here lived the sawmill magnate James T. Ryan, who owned Eclypse, the finest horse in the region and a natural attraction for Sam. The luster of a visitation was brightened by the fact that Ryan always kept a barrel of whisky on tap for the officers. This was reminiscent of more pleasant days when he visited the sutler while stationed at the Detroit Barracks.

Constantly on the watch for business opportunities with which he might augment his meager salary, Grant entered into a partnership with three other officers to lease the Union Hotel on Kearny Street in San Francisco, at a rental of $500 a month. It was incompetently managed as a "sort of club billiard-room," resulting in a heavy loss to the four.

He managed many sight seeing trips on horseback, one of them taking him 100 miles east of San Francisco to Knight's Ferry. Here he visited

46

CISCO.

by Henry Bill New York

8   Market Street Pier
9   California Street
10 Central Wharf
11 Catholic Church
12 Marine Telegraph
13 Argill Island

Julia's brother Lewis, who ran a ferry boat on the Stanislaus River.

As commandant of Fort Humboldt, Captain Robert C. Buchanan, a good soldier, was a disciplinarian. Life under his command at best was difficult. Sam's dissipation had come to his attention and it was just a matter of time when "Old Buck" caught up with him. One day the Paymaster was paying off the troops in the presence of Captain Buchanan and a tipsy Grant. Buchanan had his adjutant, Lieutenant Lewis Cass Hunt, place Sam in arrest with a view toward court martial. Years later, Rufe Ingalls related that Old Buck had demanded that Sam resign or stand trail. Though his friends urged him to stand trial,

confident he would be acquitted, he chose to resign. The resignation, effective July 31, 1854, carried with it a 60 day terminal leave of absence granted by Buchanan.

Sam left for San Francisco on May 6th, leaving from there, by way of Panama, for Sacketts Harbor. Unable to collect a $1,600 debt due him, he returned to New York to await a check from his father so he could go home to Bethel. His old friend, Simon Bolivar Buckner, on duty in New York, guaranteed his hotel bill and generally aided him until his funds arrived from Jesse. Within a few days all was well, for he had heard from his father and he was on his way home to Julia.

47

RECUPERATION POINT—Benicia Barracks was a few hours by sail from San Francisco at the mouth of the Sacramento River. Here the regiment rested for three weeks. 1853. Courtesy Library of Congress.

FORT BENICIA, CALIFORNIA—View to the southeast. Drawing by Hugo Hochholzer. Courtesy California State Library.

LAST COMMAND IN THE WEST—Grant's headquarters at Fort Humboldt, California. Made a captain as of August 9, 1853, he was placed in command of Company 'F'. Courtesy California State Library.

FORT VANCOUVER FROM THE NORTHWEST, 1854—Drawn by Gustavus Sohon. From United States, War Department Reports of Explorations and Surveys, to Ascertain the Most Practicable and Economic Route for a Railroad from the Mississippi River to the Pacific Ocean, vol. XII, Plate XLIV. From the Washington State Historical Society.

Chapter Six

No Security on a Farm

The reception in Bethel was no joyous one. Jesse faced a failure. Before him stood a son who, at the age of 32, was jobless, penniless and in disgrace. Yet Jesse must have realized that he had been a dutiful son who had gone to West Point because he had been told to go. It was true that Ulysses had overindulged while depressed. Though liquor was commonly employed, its use was primarily social. To lose a job because of it was inexcusable. Jesse, who had always boasted about "My Ulysses," could boast no more.

The welcome at White Haven was different. Julia, with open arms, made him forget the past. He was home and that was all that mattered. By his side was four-year-old Freddie and his two-year-old Ulysses Jr., whom the slaves called "Buck" because he had been born in the Buckeye State of Ohio. Even Colonel Dent made his welcome evident for, with most of his family away, he wanted Julia and Ulysses near him. If they would build on Julia's 60 acres adjacent to White Haven, he would advance the money for windows, doorways and finishing the interior. What more could Ulysses ask?

He had always wanted to be a farmer, and now he had his chance. With the arrival of spring, and having no money for farm implements or seed, he utilized his time in clearing the land. Cutting and hauling the cordwood on it to sell in St. Louis was his only means of raising funds. Though working hardest on cordwood, he took time to raise corn, oats and vegetables, and to square logs so they would be seasoned for the house he would build the next year.

Colonel Dent had given Julia three slaves—a cook, a housemaid and a houseman. Though Ulysses and his family lived at White Haven, and did so for a year, they were one of the subjects of discussion when neighbors met at the Sappington Post Office nearby. Whoever heard of a farmer with three house servants having to do his own field work.

Ulysses had a kindly feeling toward slaves. He had made it clear he would free his wife's slaves when he could. Unquestionably his antislavery attitude irked his father-in-law who had opposing views on the subject. Because of it Colonel Dent stimulated Ulysses into building a house of his own.

The two story house, as planned by Julia, had a hall through the middle, with the sitting room and dining room on either side and three bedrooms upstairs. The kitchen and the servants' quarters were in cabins behind the house.

SAINT LOUIS IN 1840—Showing Front Street with Mississippi River boats unloading at the levee. Building at left housed the City Fathers during their deliberations. J. C. Wild lithograph. Courtesy St. Louis Public Library.

During the construction Ulysses lived in Wishton-wish (an Indian name for Whippoorwill), the house of his brother-in-law Louis Dent who was in California. Hardly had they moved in when on July 4, 1855, Julia presented him with his daughter Ellen. Like her aunt, she was called Nellie.

Digging a celler, splitting shingles and hauling stone for a foundation and chimneys had him working overtime, but it was not until the summer of 1856 that the neighbors all came for the house-raising. After the chinks between the logs were filled with plaster, Ulysses dubbed it "Hardscrabble." There were those who thought he was taking a cynical poke at the fancy names the Dents had used to designate their homes.

Firewood was a certain source of sale in nearby St. Louis. Though wood was plentiful on his farm, Ulysses had discovered that someone had been cutting and carrying wood from it. Watching one night, he observed a burly fellow who rented a farm nearby, cutting up and loading one of his trees. By a short cut he headed him off, stopped him and asked what his price was for the load of wood. "About four dollars," was the reply. "I'll take it; bring it over to my house." "No. I promised it to a man in St. Louis." "No," said Grant, "you'll haul this load to my house and then pay me $20 for what you have cut and hauled away, which makes it about half price." "If I don't I suppose you will sue me before the squire?" "No, we won't trouble him but will settle it right here." With this he

seized the huge man by the coat. The man quickly shouted, "I'll do it, but don't say a word to anyone." Grant got his wood and his money.

From time to time he would meet old army acquaintances and classmates in St. Louis who would be shocked at his rundown appearance. When hauling wood he was dressed for the occasion —a stubby, sandy beard, crushed felt hat, muddy boots and a faded blue army overcoat from which the insignia had been removed.

Things were still going badly for him in the latter part of 1856. He urgently needed $500 for farm implements and his spring seed. He wrote to his father for it on several occasions, and offering to pay 10 per cent for the loan, but he received no response. That winter he cleared over ten acres of land and cut 300 cords of wood. The summer that followed was a difficult one because the nation was in the throes of a panic. Ulysses' corn and oats yielded well but had no market; his wheat yielded but 75 of the expected 500 bushels.

There was only one way he could provide his three children and pregnant wife with a happy Christmas season—pawn his gold hunting watch and chain. And he did just that. His present was another son. His fourth child, Jesse Root Grant Jr., was born February 6, 1858.

When spring arrived, Colonel Dent decided to move into St. Louis. He had only his daughter Emmy with him for his wife had passed away January 4, 1857. Things looked better for Ulysses now that he had rented White Haven and the farm

51

St. Louis.

ST. LOUIS IN 1847—Lithographed by Henry Lewis. Courtesy St. Louis Public Library.

from his father-in-law. With three Negro farmhands to assist him and a depression near its end, his future seemed secure.

Then adversity struck again. An unseasonable June cold spell crippled his crops. Following that, Freddy came down with a typhoid infection that almost took his life. Seven slaves took ill, then Julia and Ulysses came down with the ague and fever.

Early in October he wrote his father that he and Mr. Dent were selling off their stock, renting the cleared land and selling 400 acres. It was physically impossible to continue to farm, for his ague stayed with him. He had to find work of a lighter nature that would have some assurance of an adequate income.

Colonel Dent knew just the occupation. St. Louis was growing by leaps and bounds. In such a community there were bound to be many real estate transactions. He would contact his nephew,

Harry Boggs, who had such offices in St. Louis.

Dent was persuasive for Grant was taken in as a partner January 1, 1859.

Ulysses occupied an unfurnished room in the back of the Boggs house at 209 South Fifteenth Street, walking 12 miles to and from White Haven each weekend to be with his family. During the first four months he was somewhat incapacitated by daily attacks of ague, yet managed to be a diligent rent collector. In other business matters he showed little interest, perhaps because of a lowered vitality resulting from his chronic illness.

He purchased a frame cottage at the corner of Ninth and Barton in July, and it was here he moved his family. By August he realized that the partnership would have to dissolve. There was insufficient business on which two families could live.

Hearing of the need for a Superintendent of County Roads, he applied. The $1,500 a year job was given to another principally because the other man was better known as an engineer, and Grant was considered a Democrat. Grant's friends then obtained for him an appointment as a clerk in the United States Customhouse. Less than two months later the Collector of Customs died and Grant was out of his job.

With nothing left to do but visit his father in Covington, he set out for home. Jesse turned the matter over to Simpson, for he was the Galena store manager, though in Covington because of illness. Ulysses was to move to Galena and work with Orvil for $50 a month, and at the end of a year he would acquire an interest in the business should he prove valuable to it.

Arriving in Galena in April of 1860 on the steamer *Itasca* with his wife and family, he moved his furniture into a rented brick house high on the bluff overlooking the levee of the Galena River. The leathergoods firm of J. R. Grant was located at 145 Main Street, several hundred wooden steps below.

Grant's experience as a quartermaster was expected to be of value to the firm. He managed the books, and bought and weighed hides, but was an indifferent salesman. Occasionally he would make an eight to ten day trip through Wisconsin

and Iowa buying hides. For recreation he would while away his leisure hours playing euchre, whist and chess while he smoked his clay pipe. Between games he would amuse his friends with incidents of the Mexican War. Though he did not belong to the Methodist church, Julia was a member, and both attended regularly.

At that time a lively community of 14,000, Galena was the shipping center for the surrounding lead mines. It was located on the Galena River three miles from the Mississippi River. The Grants used its transporation facilities to ship raw hides to their down-river tanneries, the boats returning with finished leather for sale in their leathergoods store.

Since the day Ulysses left Fort Humboldt there had been no indication that he would return to his former habit. Though the opportunities were many while meeting, as he often did, companions of his military life, he was never known to touch a drop of liquor. The same was true in Galena though there were some who said he would take an occasional drink with friends in the evening, though usually he would take a cigar instead. One glance at the steep wooden stairs he had to climb to reach his residence would be evidence enough an intoxicated person could never make it home.

WHITE HAVEN ON GRAVOIS ROAD
—Purchased by Frederick Dent in 1821, its south wing (left) was a log cabin sometime after 1796. The main section was built of oak and walnut by slave labor in 1808. Courtesy Missouri Historical Society.

HARD SCRABBLE—Built in the Sappington neighborhood by Grant and the neighbors, all logs had been cut and hauled by Ulysses. At a log-raising bee it had been built "log laid upon log by friendly hands." In 1855 this was a fatiguing affair. Available for the needy was "extract of corn, **acqua pura sup. et lib.** as required—all appreciating this cure-all." Courtesy Library of Congress.

St. Louis, Dec 23rd 1857

I this day consign to J. S. FRELIGH, at my own risk from loss or damage by thieves or fire, to sell on commission, price not limited, *1 Gold Hunting Detached Lever & Gold chain*

on which said Freligh has advanced *Twenty Two* Dollars. And I hereby fully authorize and empower said Freligh to sell at public or private sale the above mentioned property to pay said advance—if the same is not paid to said Freligh, or these conditions renewed by paying charges, on or before *Jan 23/58*

U. S. Grant

WHEN CASH WAS SHORT—Whether Ulysses needed cash for Christmas two days later or a layette for six weeks later has not been determined. Money he sorely needed or he would not have pawned his prized hunting watch though he had a year in which to redeem it. Courtesy Illinois State Historical Society.

A BOGGS & GRANT BUSINESS CARD—Little chance had Boggs with Grant as his partner. Courtesy Missouri Historical Society.

THE CABIN THAT SAM BUILT—His only daughter Ellen (Nellie) was born in this cabin on July 4, 1855. In front of "Hardscrabble" from left to right are, C. F. Blanke, General Fred Grant, and Lieutenant Morley.

GALENA, GRANT'S HOME TOWN—
Taken from a stereo about 1865.
Courtesy Chicago Historical Society.

GRANT AND PERKINS LEATHER STORE—Jesse Grant formed a partnership with E. A. Collins in 1841 to tan and sell leather. Collins went to Galena that same year to open their leathergoods store. In 1853 they dissolved their partnership amicably, Jesse moving to a store down the street while Collins retained the old stand. In the spring of 1860 Ulysses joined the Galena staff of J. R. Grant, leaving for the service in 1861. Samuel Simpson Grant died of tuberculosis that fall leaving the store in the hands of Orvil. Orvil formed a partnership with C. R. Perkins around 1863 and bought out E. A. Collins. From a stereo, courtesy Chicago Historical Society.

GALENA FROM THE SOUTHEAST—Beginning as a lead mining and trading center in the 1820s its location, some six miles from the Mississippi River, permitted considerable river traffic with St. Louis. From an 1856 Whitefield lithograph. Courtesy Illinois State Historical Library.

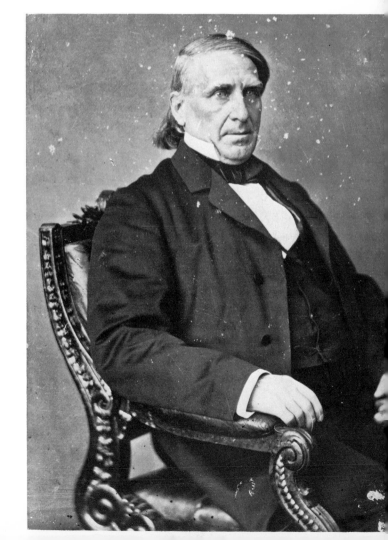

CONGRESSMAN ELIHU B. WASHBURNE OF ILLINOIS—Washburne, a native of Galena, took a liking to Grant and used his influence to obtain unsought promotions for him. To Washburne alone goes the credit for the early recognition of Grant's ability. Brady photo courtesy Library of Congress.

GALENA LEVEE—From a Daguerreotype by Alexander Hesler about 1852. Courtesy Chicago Historical Society.

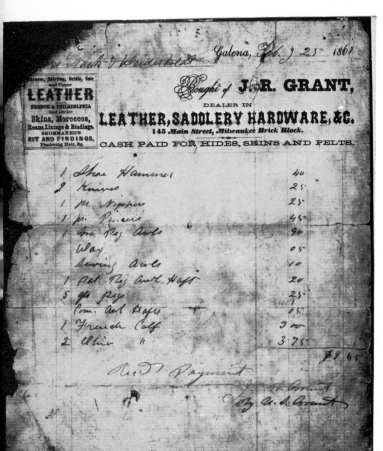

ULYSSES EARNS HIS KEEP—Invoice made out to a cobbler by U. S. Grant, February 15, 1861. Original in Galena Historical Museum and reproduced courtesy Galena Historical Society.

FIRST HOME IN GALENA—Grant and his family arrived in Galena, Illinois, in April of 1860. They lived in this brick house at 121 South High Street, well above the business district. The rent was $100 a year. Courtesy Chicago Historical Society.

Grant's Galena home during the War

PACKET BOAT DOCKED AT GALENA—A sidewheeler very similar to the packet **ITASKA** that brought Grant and his family to Galena. From a Daguerreotype taken by Alexander Hesler in 1854. Courtesy Chicago Historical Society.

GOVERNOR RICHARD YATES OF ILLINOIS—Yates, through the insistance of Washburne and other important political personages, offered Grant the colonelcy of the Seventh District Regiment. He never regretted it. Courtesy Library of Congress.

MAJOR GENERAL GEORGE B. McCLELLAN—"Little Mac" McClellan was idolized by his soldiers but not by an over-patient President. Overcautious and slow to the point of exasperation, Lincoln removed him from command. Courtesy Library of Congress.

JEFFERSON DAVIS — PRESIDENT OF THE CONFEDERACY — A graduate of West Point in 1828, he served in the war with Mexico, declining the rank of brigadier general to become a member of the U. S. Senate from Mississippi. Courtesy Library of Congress.

Chapter Seven

Prelude for a Brigadier

The Northern and Southern states were in an economic contest. With the North attracting the majority of the immigrants and industry, and the South becoming predominantly agricultural on a basis of slave labor, a population explosion in the North gave it a predominance of votes in the House of Representatives. The South, in order to equalize matters, realized it must retain or obtain its share of states in order to balance the power in the Senate.

Many compromises had been attempted to maintain an equality, yet the North, led by reformers, fanatic editors and unrealistic politicians, created a feeling that slavery must be abolished. This was resented in the South even though many knew it would soon have to end. They, however, wanted to reserve the right to end it in their own way. Pressed and harassed by the North, their bitterness and hostility increased to the breaking point. Then came the split.

There was a flurry in Galena on April 15, 1861, for word had just been received at the telegraph office that Fort Sumter had fallen. Jefferson Davis, President of the Confederate States of America, had demanded the withdrawal of Federal troops from it, without effect. Then he had taken stronger measures.

Galena's reaction to the stunning news was a public meeting in the second floor courtroom. With attorney Charles S. Hempstead presiding, the meeting reached the peak of its patriotic fervor when attorney John A. Rawlins addressed the packed assembly. Ulysses, who had never heard a speech of this nature and never forgot it, said to Orvil on the way home, "I think I ought to go into the service." And Orvil agreed.

Several nights later, at a meeting at the courthouse, Ulysses was made chairman by acclamation. Shyly indicating that the purpose of the meeting was to recruit, he stumbled through the evening, ending it with several dozen volunteers.

In a short time there were over 80 recruits. When the time arrived to elect officers, Ulysses was asked to accept command of the newly organized Jo Daviess Guards, but refused. Yet he offered to serve the company in every way he could.

Congressman Elihu B. Washburne and his friends pressed Grant to go to Springfield with the newly mobilized volunteers, to which he assented. The troops were stationed at Camp Yates, in the suburbs of Springfield, on April 26th. Two days later, while turning over the Jo Daviess Guards to Governor Richard Yates, he offered his own services. The Governor indicated there was nothing for him at that time. The following day, when introduced by the Governor

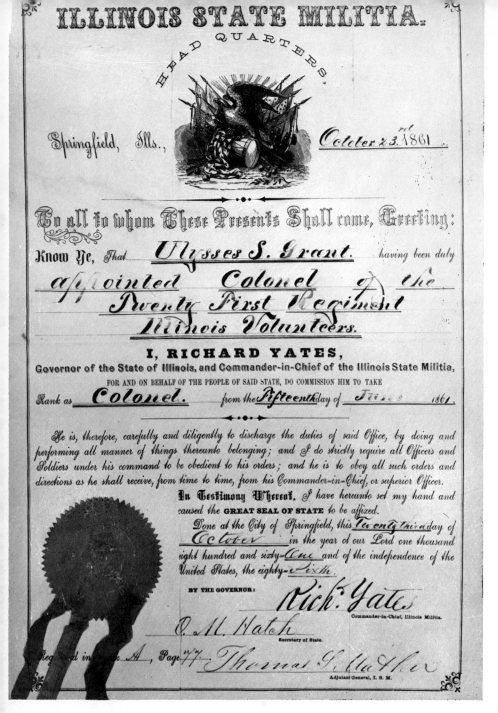

ILLINOIS STATE MILITIA.

HEAD QUARTERS.

Springfield, Ills., *October 23rd 1861*

To all to whom These Presents Shall come, Greeting:

Know Ye, That *Ulysses S. Grant* having been duly *appointed Colonel of the Twenty First Regiment Illinois Volunteers.*

I, RICHARD YATES,

Governor of the State of Illinois, and Commander-in-Chief of the Illinois State Militia,

FOR AND ON BEHALF OF THE PEOPLE OF SAID STATE, DO COMMISSION HIM TO TAKE

Rank as *Colonel.* from the *Fifteenth* day of *June* 1861.

He is, therefore, carefully and diligently to discharge the duties of said Office, by doing and performing all manner of things thereunto belonging; and I do strictly require all Officers and Soldiers under his command to be obedient to his orders; and he is to obey all such orders and directions as he shall receive, from time to time, from his Commander-in-Chief, or superior Officer.

In Testimony Whereof, I have hereunto set my hand and caused the **GREAT SEAL OF STATE** to be affixed.

Done at the City of Springfield, this *Twenty third* day of *October* in the year of our Lord one thousand eight hundred and sixty-*One* and of the independence of the United States, the eighty-*Sixth.*

BY THE GOVERNOR:

Rich. Yates
Commander-in-Chief, Illinois Militia.

O. M. Hatch
Secretary of State.

Registered in Book A, Page 77. *Thomas S. Mather*
Adjutant General, I. S. M.

CAPTAIN TO COLONEL—Made a captain of the Fourth U. S. Infantry August 5, 1854, Grant became a colonel of the 21st Illinois Volunteers on June 15, 1861. Courtesy The Smithsonian Institution.

to Colonel Mather, the Adjutant General, he was given some clerical work to do. It soon was evident he was the only one in the office with any military background.

Governor Yates discovered that Captain John Pope, his commander at Camp Yates, had departed for St. Louis in a huff for not having been elected Brigadier General. On May 4th he appointed Grant to succeed him. Eager to obtain a command of his own, for his principal duties at Camp Yates were only those of drillmaster and mustering-in officer, Grant was becoming depressed in spirits for want of the chance.

On May 22nd Yates gave him a leave. While in Galena two days later, he wrote to the Adjutant General in Washington giving his background and tendering his services for military command. Returning to Springfield and finding nothing to do, and with no answer from Washington, he requested and received a week's leave to visit his parents in Covington. Once there he quickly crossed the river to Cincinnati to visit Major General George B. McClellan who was organizing the Ohio Volunteers. Two successive days of calling offered no opportunity of seeing him. McClellan could not be bothered.

Back in Galena on June 15th Grant found a telegram from Yates offering him the colonelcy of the Seventh District Regiment, whose men would not re-enlist unless the vain and tipsy Colonel Simon S. Goode was replaced. Within a short time afterward another telegram arrived offering him the colonelcy of the Twelfth Ohio. The White boys, Carr and Chilton, knowing his story, had been working in his behalf. Grant had to reject the second offer for he already had accepted the first.

Grant's presence in camp soon brought order to the undisciplined regiment. But June 28th was the day of decision. The regiment which had boasted 1,250 men had shrunk to little over 600 and the time was arriving when they would decide whether they would leave or re-enlist.

Two Democratic Congressmen were brought in to inspire the men—John A. Logan and John A. McClernand. The troops were assembled at the State Fairgrounds, which formed Fort Yates, McClernand being introduced first. Each gave ample evidence of his oratorical skill but it was Logan whose eloquence, patriotic fervor and logic won the day. When he concluded, 603 men volunteered. And when the applause died away and the new Colonel Grant was presented, there were cries of "Speech! Speech!" As he stepped forward he gave them one they talked of for days. In a low, clear and penetrating voice he issued a command: "Men, go to your quarters!" And they did.

On mustering in, the old regiment became the 21st Illinois Volunteers. They were an unruly lot but in a week's time much of the roughness had been scraped off. Grant's method was simple—he was rougher than any one of them.

Leaving Springfield on foot, for Grant wanted his men to absorb more discipline, the regiment moved on to Quincy. Crossing the Mississippi in mid-July, Grant led his men through enemy territory in search of the Confederate Colonel Thomas Harris and his band of marauders. After a few days of marching over rough Missouri roads, in which much was learned about handling a regiment in the field, he came upon the recently held camp of the rebel raider. He had approached the camp with a palpitating heart to find Harris had left in haste. It occurred to him that Harris

had been as afraid of him as he had been of Harris, thereby learning a valuable lesson.

The 21st Illinois moved on to Mexico, Missouri, where it encamped until the middle of August. After Grant had been its Colonel about a month, notice arrived that he had been made a brigadier general. With a large Volunteer Army being created, over 30 brigadier generals were needed. The President had allocated four for Illinois, permitting the Illinois Congressional Delegation to name them. Congressman Elihu B. Washburne who, with Governor Yates, had kept a watchful eye on Grant, had thrown his considerable political weight around in Grant's favor. The others named from Illinois were Stephen A. Hurlburt, John A. McClernand and Benjamin M. Prentiss. Confirmed by the Senate on August 5th, his appointment was effective retroactively as of May 17, 1861.

Thinking it proper that one of his aids should come from his regiment, Grant appointed Lieutenant Clark B. Lagow. Grant also wanted

MAJOR GENERAL JOHN CHARLES FRÉMONT—As a famous explorer and scientist, the first presidential candidate of the Republican party (1856), this patriot took command of the Western Department. He was poor as a soldier and worse as an executive though by November, 1861, he had raised 56,000 troops. Frémont liked Grant's "self-poise, modesty, decision, attention to details." Courtesy Library of Congress.

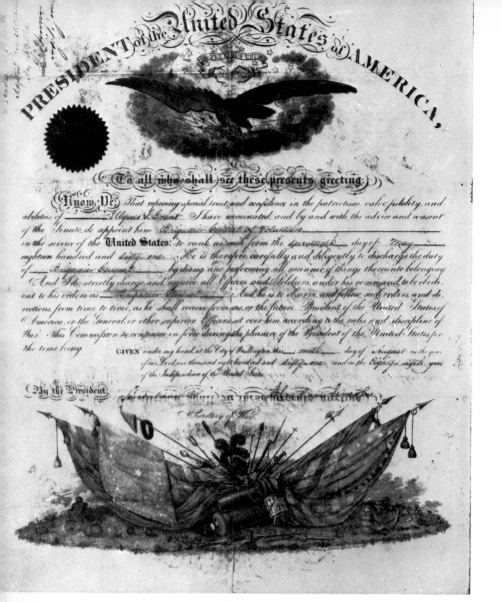

ONCE A GENERAL—Technically a general before he was a colonel, this commission signed by Abraham Lincoln and dated August 9, 1861, making Grant a brigadier general of Volunteers, was retroactive to May 17, 1861. Courtesy The Smithsonian Institution.

some representation from Galena on his staff. Remembering the stirring oratory of attorney John A. Rawlins, he wrote offering him the position of Assistant Adjutant General with the rank of captain. Rawlins rejected the rank of major in a newly organized regiment to accept. Perhaps Grant felt a need for geographic association. His next appointment was W. S. Hillyer, in whose St. Louis law office Grant had a desk while in the real estate business.

After the addle-pated Major General John C. Frémont had straightened out the mixup of Grant's plans, having placed Brigadier General Prentiss over Grant when Grant ranked him, he ordered Grant to establish a command post for the District of Southeast Missouri at Cairo. Reaching there September 4th, Grant found himself writing to Congressman Washburne: "Allow me to thank you for the part you have taken in giving me my present

position. . . . My whole heart is in the cause we are fighting for. . . . and you shall never have cause to regret the part you have taken."

The following day one of Frémont's scouts reported to him that Confederate General Leonidas Polk had sent General Gideon Pillow with a sizable force of unknown numbers to occupy Hickman and the bluffs of Columbus, Kentucky. It was evident Kentucky no longer would be neutral. Grant sent a dispatch to Frémont that unless he got orders to the contrary he was going to occupy the town of Paducah. Receiving none within the next few hours, he prepared his move.

Both Paducah and Cairo were strategically important. Cairo, at the juncture of the Ohio with the Mississippi River, and Paducah, 45 miles up the Ohio on the Kentucky side near the junctions of both the Tennessee and Cumberland Rivers, controlled pathways to the interior of some of the most important states in the Confederacy.

The War Department had purchased three river boats at Cincinnati, the *Lexington, Conestoga* and *Tyler*. Each was armed with smooth-bore 32 and 64 pound cannon, protected by five inch oak bulwarks, and manned by the Navy under Army jurisdiction. James B. Eads of St. Louis had been ordered to construct seven gunboats covered with metal sheathing, but these would not be ready for this endeavor.

With the three gunboats, the 9th and 12th Illinois Regiments loaded on transports, and with a four gun battery of field artillery Grant took off that evening, reaching the Paducah waterfront at dawn. Meeting no opposition, for the rebel troops had not arrived, he proceeded with the orderly occupation of an unsympathetic city. It was then he learned that 4,000 Confederate troops were three hours away. They had turned back on learning of his occupation. He had taken Paducah without firing a shot.

In early November word came through that the Confederate forces at Columbus, Kentucky, were to be reinforced. At dawn of the 7th Grant's men were able to disembark at Belmont, across the Mississippi River from Columbus. Meeting their equal in numbers, some 2,700, they drove the rebel forces from their camp to the river, in a complete rout. The urge and desire for spoils and the exultation of victory caused the men to cast aside all caution and discipline. With the opening of the batteries at Columbus, General Polk and his officers rallied their men and counter-attacked, causing

ADMIRAL ANDREW H. FOOTE— As a Flag Officer, Foote, on the gunboat **Cincinnati** opened the engagement at the battle of Fort Henry. After an hour of his bombardment the flag of the fort was lowered in surrender. At the arrival of Grant's forces an hour later, Foote turned over the fort to Grant. Courtesy Library of Congress.

GRANT AT CAIRO, ILLINOIS, SEPTEMBER 1861—Yet an unknown, Grant had his headquarters at the St. Charles Hotel. He stands in the middle with his right hand in his pocket next to Gen. McClernand, who is in front of the pillar. Standing on each side are townspeople. Courtesy Chicago Historical Society.

GRANT'S INDISPENSABLE MAN—John A. Rawlins, a Galena attorney, was appointed captain and assistant adjutant general on Grant's first staff. Conscientious, loyal, industrious, with a good mind, he was a teetotaler who held a firm leash on Grant's drinking tendencies. Grant, who never used profanity, said, "I always disliked hearing anybody swear except Rawlins." Rawlins rose to the rank of major general and became Grant's chief of staff. He was Grant's first Secretary of War. Taken at Cairo, Illinois, October, 1861. Courtesy Library of Congress.

the Union soldiers to become panic-stricken. When the men began to cry out that they were surrounded, Grant said they had cut their way in and they could cut their way out just as easily. After fighting their way back to the boats, Grant was the last to go aboard. A victory had turned into a retreat. It might have been a rout but for the steady, experienced hand of Grant.

Major General Henry W. Halleck replaced General Frémont with himself on November 9th, just two days after the battle. From then until early February, 1862, Grant and his men had little to do. He utilized the time preparing his men for the struggle he knew to be ahead.

Grant realized that with the Cumberland and Tennessee Rivers in the hands of the North, the South would be compelled to withdraw from the State of Kentucky. Possession of Forts Henry and Donelson would be necessary, and to accomplish

this he had a plan. Receiving permission, he visited Halleck at his St. Louis headquarters where his presentation was cut short as if it had been preposterous.

Grant then consulted with Flag Officer Andrew H. Foote, who commanded the gunboat fleet in the area under Halleck's jurisdiction. Both agreed to the campaign up the Tennessee, and both coordinated their requests to Halleck for permission to take Fort Henry. Halleck consented, and the expedition started out on February 2nd.

Brigadier General Charles F. Smith commanded the troops on the west bank of the Tennessee, and Grant took charge of those on the east bank. The armies marched forward on both sides as the Navy flotilla under Foote bombarded Fort Henry.

The naval victory was unexpectedly easy, the garrisons of Fort Henry and the unfinished Fort Heiman across the river retreating before the Union troops arrived. Fort Henry surrendered to Foote who turned it over to Grant when he arrived.

The retreating rebel forces headed for Fort

CAPTAIN WILLIAM S. HILLYER—An aide-de-camp on Grant's first staff, he had been a member of the St. Louis law firm of McClellan, Hillyer & Moody where Grant had desk space while in the real estate business. Taken at Cairo, October, 1861. Courtesy Library of Congress.

troops that were amply supplied. Their division broke and fled, yet there were boxes of ammunition nearby that had not been issued to them.

Hearing some of the men say that the enemy had come out with their knapsacks filled with rations, Grant reasoned they were attempting to get out with their entire force but had to fall back. He decided to begin an assault on the left of the line at once. Taking a member of his staff, Colonel J. D. Webster with him, he called out to the disorganized men as they rode along the line, telling them to fill their cartridge boxes and get into line as the enemy were trying to escape. The men responded immediately. General C. F. Smith was informed of the situation and ordered to attack with his entire division. Smith had most of his men within the enemy lines in short order, there to bivouac for the night of the 15th.

That night the Confederate officers held a council of war. All agreed there was no possibility of holding the fort any longer. The commanding officer, General Floyd, had been Secretary of War

CAPTAIN CLARK B. LAGOW—Grant appointed Lieutenant Lagow from the regiment he commanded thinking it proper that one of his aides-de-camp should come from it. Taken at Cairo, October 1861. Courtesy Library of Congress.

DR. JAMES SIMONS—Selected by Grant to be the Medical Director of the District. Taken at Cairo, October, 1861. Courtesy Library of Congress.

Donelson 11 miles away, Grant following them with deliberation and caution across the narrow neck of land that separated the two forts. Facing a rebel force of 21,000 led by three Confederate generals, John B. Floyd, Gideon J. Pillow and his old friend Simon B. Buckner, on February 14th Grant watched Foote's flotilla unsuccessfully assault Donelson.

Returning afterward from a visit to the wounded Foote aboard his flagship, Grant was met by Captain Hillyer of his staff who informed him that his right flank had been smashed by a Confederate attempt to break through the Union lines toward Nashville. Grant rode over the frozen ground toward the point of disaster, noticing in passing, that the left and center of his lines were in good condition. When he reached the right he discovered "the enemy had come out in full force to cut his way out and make his escape." Brigadier General John A. McClernand's men had borne the brunt of the attack until their ammunition ran out without which they could not stand up against

PROCLAMATION,
TO THE CITIZENS OF
PADUCAH!

I have come among you, not as an enemy, but as your friend and fellow-citizen, not to injure or annoy you, but to respect the rights, and to defend and enforce the rights of all loyal citizens. An enemy, in rebellion against our common Government, has taken possession of, and planted its guns upon the soil of Kentucky and fired upon our flag. Hickman and Columbus are in his hands. He is moving upon your city. I am here to defend you against this enemy and to assert and maintain the authority and sovereignty of your Government and mine. I have nothing to do with opinions. I shall deal only with armed rebellion and its aiders and abetors. You can pursue your usual avocations without fear or hindrance. The strong arm of the Government is here to protect its friends, and to punish only its enemies. Whenever it is manifest that you are able to defend yourselves, to maintain the authority of your Government and protect the rights of all its loyal citizens, I shall withdraw the forces under my command from your city.

U. S. GRANT,
Brig. Gen. U. S. A., Commanding.
Paducah, Sept 6th. 1861.

GRANT TAKES PADUCAH—When Grant learned that General Leonidas Polk had violated Kentucky's voluntary neutrality by his occupation of Columbus, he quickly occupied Paducah encountering no resistance. That his troops were unwelcome was evident. To counteract this feeling he had these broadsides posted around the town. Courtesy The Ohio Historical Society.

THORN IN THE SIDE—Lieutenant General Henry Wager Halleck was general-in-chief from July, 1862 to March, 1864, when Grant took command of the armies. Gideon Welles wrote: "Halleck originates nothing; anticipates nothing; takes no responsibility; suggests nothing; is good for nothing." Courtesy Library of Congress.

but never had been a soldier. He had left his office with a cloud over his head and did not want to be captured. Hence he yielded his command to General Pillow. Pillow said he too would not stay. It was up to Buckner to assume the distasteful task, which he did by assuming command.

Before daylight of February 16th, under a flag of truce, Buckner sent a message to Grant suggesting that commissioners be appointed to discuss the terms of surrender. Grant replied: "No terms except an unconditional and immediate surrender can be accepted. I propose to move immediately upon your works." Buckner accepted the terms.

There were nearly 15,000 prisoners as against Grant's forces now reinforced to 21,000. With the prisoners went 65 guns and over 17,000 small arms. This unforeseen victory opened the Confederacy from the Appalachian Mountains to the Mississippi River. The news caused great rejoicing all over the North, for this was its first major victory. Grant's terms of capitulation were the topics of discussion everywhere, soon earning him the nickname of "Unconditional Surrender" Grant.

It was not Grant's wish to humiliate his prisoners. He told Buckner they could keep their personal baggage and the officers their sidearms, but all horses and public property must be given up.

In discussing the recent events, Buckner told him: "If I had been in command, you wouldn't have reached Fort Donelson so easily." Grant replied: "If you had been in command, I should have waited for reinforcements, and marched from Fort Henry in greater strength; but I knew that Pillow would not come out of the works to fight, and told my staff so, though I believed he would fight behind his works."

TAKING FORT HENRY—Grant and Foote agreed upon a joint army and navy attack. The task force consisted of the ironclads **Carondelet, Cincinnati, Essex**, and **St. Louis** and the timberclads **Conestoga, Lexington**, and **Tyler** with a number of transports. This is a typical gunboat. Courtesy Chicago Historical Society.

GUNBOAT AND TRANSPORT—Anchored opposite Cairo, Illinois, these boats were useful in the offenses of the west. 1864. Courtesy Chicago Historical Society.

CARONDELET—An ironclad gunboat that saw heavy service against river fortresses. Engraving by Samuel Sartain from a J. Hamilton drawing. Courtesy Chicago Historical Society.

GRANT'S HAT ORNAMENT WORN AT FORT DONELSON—February 6, 1862. Courtesy The Smithsonian Institution.

WOODCLAD RIVERBOAT—This timber protected riverboat, the **U.S.S. Cricket,** was typical of the Mississippi mercantile fleet converted to military use. Courtesy Library of Congress.

STORMING OF FORT DONELSON—On February 16, 1862 the fort surrendered to Grant's "Unconditional Surrender" terms. Currier and Ives print, courtesy Nationwide Insurance.

GENEROUS ENEMY—General Simon Bolivar Buckner, an old friend and West Point schoolmate, was held in high esteem by Grant. He surrendered the Confederate garrison of Fort Donelson to Grant when his superiors Generals J. B. Floyd and Gideon J. Pillow ran out on him. Courtesy Library of Congress.

GENERAL BUCKNER'S REQUEST AT FORT DONELSON—The brave Buckner was left to his own devices by Generals Floyd and Pillow. Courtesy The National Archives.

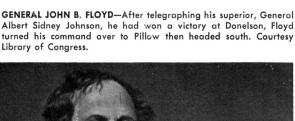

GRANT DEMANDED AN UNCONDITIONAL SURRENDER—Though West Point classmates and friends, this was war. Courtesy The National Archives.

GREAT CONFEDERATE CAVALRY LEADER—General Nathan Bedford Forrest was a lieutenant colonel when he escaped from Fort Donelson across an icy stream with about 500 cavalrymen. Courtesy Library of Congress.

GENERAL JOHN B. FLOYD—After telegraphing his superior, General Albert Sidney Johnson, he had won a victory at Donelson, Floyd turned his command over to Pillow then headed south. Courtesy Library of Congress.

NO LOVE LOST—General Gideon J. Pillow was one Confederate officer Grant disliked. He remembered him with disrespect for his Mexican service and for his inglorious retreat from Fort Donelson. Courtesy of Library of Congress.

BATTLE OF SHILOH—April 6-7, 1862. Grant wrote that: "Shiloh was the severest battle fought in the West during the war, and but few in the East equalled it for hard, determined fighting." Currier and Ives print. Courtesy Nationwide Insurance.

PITTSBURG LANDING—SHILOH—Buell's troops crossing the Tennesee River to support Grant. Gunboats **Tyler** and **Lexington** in the middle. Drawing by Henri Lovie. Courtesy New York Public Library, Prints Division.

Chapter Eight

I Can't Spare This Man

Prior to Fort Donelson, Grant had been a pipe smoker—a clay pipe while working in the Galena leathergoods store, a meerschaum pipe with an 8 or 10 inch curved stem following the increase in income as a general. The newspapers had represented him as smoking an unlit cigar during the course of the Donelson battle. The result was a constant flow of boxes of choice cigars. Giving away the bigger share of them but left with a large quantity, he thought it a shame to let them go to waste. The cigar habit became a permanent one.

After receiving Grant's victory message February 17th Halleck wired McClellan: "Make Buell, Grant and Pope major generals of volunteers and give me command in the west. I ask this for Forts Henry and Donelson." Two days later he requested a major general's commission for C. F. Smith. No real reason was given for including Buell and Pope in the promotions. Neither Secretary of War Edwin M. Stanton nor General-in-Chief George B. McClellan was taken in by the combined request. President Lincoln sent one name to the Senate for confirmation—U. S. Grant. He was made a major general of volunteers effective February 16, 1862.

"Old Brains" Halleck persisted in his demands for top command of the armies in the west. McClellan had his own problems in getting what he wanted. He discovered that Halleck was not familiar with either the numbers of troops or their disposition, so more information was requested. On March 3rd Halleck wired McClellan: "I have had no communication with General Grant for more than a week. He left his command without my authority and went to Nashville. . . . I can get no returns, no reports, no information of any kind from him. Satisfied with his victory, he sits down and enjoys it without any regard for the future."

McClellan's response stated: "Generals must observe discipline as well as private soldiers. Do not hesitate to arrest him at once if the good of the service requires it, and place C. F. Smith in command. . . ."

On the following day Halleck wired McClellan that he had received a rumor that Grant "had resumed his former bad habits" which accounted for his neglect. And on that same day he ordered Grant to remain at Fort Henry, and placed Major General Smith in charge of the expedition. In this same message he asked why Grant did not obey orders to report strength and positions of his command. This was all news to Grant for he had been sending daily messages to Halleck.

Remorsefully, he realized he was tied to Fort Henry while Smith would take command of

ABLE ENGINEER—When Grant left his Western army to take over full command of the armies he wrote Sherman: "I want to express my thanks to you and to McPherson, as the men to whom, above all others, I feel indebted for whatever I have had of success." James Birdseye McPherson commanded a corps at Vicksburg. Courtesy Library of Congress.

I wish you as soon as your new army is in the field to assume the immediate command and lead it on to new victories."

Later, the telegraph operator at the Cairo end of the wire deserted, taking with him all of the dispatches. He was proven to be a rebel who had intercepted both the Grant and Halleck messages, thereby creating the uncomfortable situation.

Resuming command on March 17th, Grant discovered half his army at Savannah, on the east bank of the Tennessee River, and the balance on the west bank distributed between Crump's Landing and Pittsburg Landing, less than 10 miles above Savannah. The enemy had concentrated at the vital rail center of Corinth, some 20 miles away. Possession of this center would deprive the rebel forces of transportation for military supplies and men. Strategically it was vital to Grant's future plans.

An injury to General Smith's leg at this time, that ultimately was fatal, forced him to give up his command. Grant began a concentration of force at Pittsburg Landing while awaiting Halleck's arrival to take personal command of his and the advancing forces under Major General Don Buell. Though Grant waited, the Confederate forces did not.

MAJOR GENERAL DON CARLOS BUELL—Halleck had given him a separate command at Shiloh placing Grant in a delicate position when it came to issuing commands. Grant treated him as an equal. Courtesy Library of Congress.

the forces in the field. He had no feeling against Smith, nothing but the highest respect and admiration, for he had been commandant of cadets at West Point when Grant had been there. It wasn't easy to remain inactive when he knew his men were preparing for action against Corinth, and he was not to be with him.

Halleck continued to reprimand Grant with telegrams charging him with "going to Nashville without authority," with having "created great dissatisfaction and seriously interfered with military plans" and with alleged irregularities in the handling of captured food and weapons. Grant's anger was evident when he wired Halleck: "There is such a disposition to find fault with me that I again ask to be relieved from further duty until I can be placed right in the estimation of those in higher authority."

This near-request for an unwelcome court of inquiry, coupled with the removal of McClellan as commander of the army and a directive from the President to investigate the allegations against Grant, caused Halleck to telegraph him: "You cannot be relieved from your command .There is no good reason for it. . . . instead of relieving you

Early in the morning of April 6th, a skirmish line of General William J. Hardee encountered a reconnoitering party under Union Major James E. Powell, forcing it to retreat. A general engagement resulted in the area of Shiloh Church, several miles from Pittsburg Landing. It was this small log Methodist meeting-house that gave the battle its name.

Several days before, Grant's horse had slipped under him on ground soggy from several days of rain. Grant's leg received the entire weight of the animal's body, resulting in a severe ankle sprain. For several days he had to resort to crutches. While breakfasting in Savannah on April 6th, he heard the cannonading of the battle of Shiloh. When he reached the scene of battle it was 10 a.m. and his troops were heavily engaged.

The engagements of the next few days were centered on the log church, since it was considered the key position. In the two days of severe fighting that followed, there were countless charges and countercharges, both Union and Confederate, resulting in a slowly advancing Union line. Confederate commander General Albert Sidney Johnston was mortally wounded when he ignored a severed artery in his right leg and bled to death,

POLITICAL GENERAL—Major General John Alexander McClernand, a former Democratic Congressman from Illinois, was not wanted by Grant because he was incompetent and insuborinate. The ambitious and energetic non-professional was relieved by Grant near Vicksburg. Courtesy Library of Congress.

MAJOR GENERAL LEWIS WALLACE—A political general, he had marched his division in the wrong direction at a time he was sorely needed by Grant. On the second day at Shiloh, June 7th, Wallace was in the action. He did much better at writing, producing "Ben Hur" after the war. Courtesy Library of Congress.

General Pierre G. T. Beauregard taking over the command. The arrival of Buell with some 17,000 troops to reinforce Grant caused Beauregard to decide it was useless prolonging an unequal struggle. The Confederate forces retired from the field by 4 p.m. Heading for Corinth, they were not harassed until the following evening when Generals Thomas J. Wood and William T. Sherman fell upon their rear at Fallen Timbers. They were put to flight by Southern cavalry commanded by Colonel Nathan Bedford Forrest.

The two-day battle was claimed as a victory by both sides. With nearly 24,000 killed, wounded or missing out of a combined total of nearly 110,000 men, the larger losses being on the Union side, neither side could celebrate. The reward was the abandonment to the North of Corinth on May 30th, thus severing the railroad between Memphis and Chattanooga.

If the Union soldiers had any thought of an easy and early victory after the fall of Forts Henry and Donelson, it was erased after the roughing-up they received at Shiloh. And the Confederate soldiers no longer could boast that any one of them was equal to 10 Feds.

Halleck arrived at Pittsburg Landing on April 11th, taking over command in person. He had notified Grant two days earlier to "avoid another battle, if you can, till all arrive. We then shall be able to beat them without fail." On April 13th

he officially thanked Grant and Buell and their soldiers for their victory, following it with a note ordering Grant to put his command in condition to resist another attack. Again Grant found himself playing second fiddle to Halleck in the field.

Meanwhile Grant was being blasted unjustly in the newspapers and criticized by politicians because of incorrect reporting of the battle and false charges of drunkenness. Colonel James H. Wilson, a member of Grant's staff, wrote of a delegation of citizens descending upon the President and counseling him on rumor that Grant had been drinking on duty. Lincoln responded with: "I can't say whether Grant is a drinking man or not, but if he is, I should like to know where he buys his liquor as I wish to present each one of my army commanders with a barrel of the same brand."

When John Fenton Long, a devoted friend of Grant's, made mention of his victories to Colonel Dent, his angry reply indicated he had no use for his Federal son-in-law nor place at his table for him, whereas his daughter Julia would always be welcome.

Halleck had written a book on strategy, a matter that made many think he was an expert. This campaign was to be his first and last time at the front during the entire war. He would show everyone how to take Corinth. Beginning a series of advances and entrenchments, he traveled 20 miles in 20 days, with 120,000 troops. Cautiously and laboriously he approached Corinth, for he did not intend to make any of the mistakes the other commanders had made preceding Shiloh. On May 30th Beauregard silently slipped out of Corinth, leaving it undefended for Halleck to occupy. Beauregard had outfoxed him.

Officials in Washington were beginning to wonder. Grant had become little more than an observer. Though he was second in command, orders from headquarters were sent to either wing without keeping him informed. His feeling of embarrassment increased, causing him to ask Halleck to relieve him. This Halleck refused to do.

GENERAL PIERRE G. T. BEAUREGARD—General Albert Sidney Johnston, commander of the Confederate troops, was killed at bloody Shiloh leaving Beauregard in command. Courtesy Library of Congress.

MR. LINCOLN GOES VISITING—On October 3, 1862, Lincoln called at Major General George B. McClellan's headquarters to determine why his campaign was not more aggressive. "Little Mac" as McClellan's men fondly called him, differed radically on the conduct of the war. McClellan faces Lincoln; Capt. G. A. Custer, McClellan's aide-de-camp on extreme right. Alexander Gardner photo, Courtesy National Archives.

Grant considered resigning; in fact, he had received permission from Halleck to leave the department. When Sherman discovered Grant's tents being taken down and his bags packed, he begged him to stay, arguing "that if he went away, events would go right along, and he would be left out, whereas if he remained, some happy accident might restore him to favor and to his true place."

Sherman and Grant had begun a long, firm friendship prior to the surrender at Fort Donelson. Sherman, though senior in rank, wrote to Grant on February 13th: "I will do everything in my power to hurry forward reinforcements and supplies; and if I could be of service myself, would gladly come, without making any question of rank with you or General (C. F.) Smith." Following the surrender, Sherman sent Grant warm congratulations when others were getting all the credit from Halleck.

Sherman convinced him to stay by showing him that the newspapers had called him crazy before the battle of Shiloh, but that single battle had given him new life.

His foresight was evident when, on July 11th, Halleck was ordered to Washington to become general-in-chief. With Halleck out of the field and Grant now commander of the department, he proceeded to gather in his large but scattered forces. They had been used ineffectively as a defense force; it was his intent to go on the offensive. Never losing sleep wondering what the enemy would be doing, he spent his waking hours working out a plan that made the enemy worry about what he was going to do. He spent the last six months of 1862 in northern Mississippi and western Tennessee.

HE WAS THERE—Henri Lovie, staff artist of **Frank Leslie's Illustrated Newspaper**, made this sketch on April 6, 1862 at Pittsburg Landing (Shiloh) and then titled it "Grant's last ditch line repulses final assault at dusk." Courtesy New York Public Library, Prints Division.

Vicksburg in Northern hands would mean complete Union possession of the Mississippi River, thereby dividing the Confederacy into two equal parts. It was to this end that Grant laid his plans. It was his opinion that ". . . the opening of the Mississippi River will be to us of more advantage than the capture of forty Richmonds."

Grant, assigned command of the Department of Tennessee on October 25th, launched a full-scale expedition against Vicksburg that December. With Lieutenant General John C. Pemberton, a West Pointer who had served with Grant in Mexico, defending the all-important objective, the first assault on December 29th failed.

The Union forces — numbering about 45,000, under corps commanders Major General John McClernand, Major General James Birdseye McPherson and General Sherman—combined with Porter's Western Flotilla consisting of 11 ironclads, 38 wooden gunboats and auxiliary craft with a complement of over 300 guns and 5,500 men.

Grant saw that it would be an arduous campaign with the accent on transportation. To land below Vicksburg one had to pass its shore batteries. Sherman's men built a canal on the peninsula opposite Vicksburg to bypass it, but were flooded out. Another such attempt, the Duckport Canal, was blocked by a falling river level.

With the Union defeat at Fredericksburg, Virginia, on December 13th and Grant's Army of the Tennessee slowed down in a wet season on the lowland above Vicksburg, Grant had his usual critics in Washington, even though he showed persistent aggressiveness.

A. K. McClure, an astute Pennsylvania politician, had advised President Lincoln the administration could ill-afford any political liabilities at that time. Grant must go. He was a drunkard and a stumble bum. After Lincoln heard him out, he was silent awhile and then replied. "I can't spare this man; he fights."

Against the advice of his officers, Grant decided to cut loose from his base of supplies on the river

THE LAST CHARGE—On the spot sketch of Henri Lovie at Pittsburg Landing, April 6, 1862. Grant was at Savannah when this battle of Shiloh began, but was present at this last charge of the Federal troops. Immediately after the battle both sides claimed a victory. Courtesy New York Public Library, Prints Division.

and attack while subsisting on the land. Moving rapidly between the forces of Pemberton and General Joe E. Johnston on May 7th, he pressed forward to win a series of five hard-fought engagements.

Testing the immediate defenses of Vicksburg by assaults on May 19th and 22nd, Grant determined a siege would be less costly. At about this same time General Robert E. Lee started his Army of Northern Virginia on its invasion that ended in the battle of Gettysburg.

The Army of Vicksburg held its line for six weeks while Grant prepared for a grand assault calculated to take place on July 6th. Pemberton, seeing his supplies dwindle and no reinforcements in sight, recognized the wisdom of capitulation. On July 3rd he presented, under flags of truce, a request for terms of surrender. Grant's answer was that of Fort Donelson—unconditional surrender.

On July 4th the gallant garrison of Vicksburg marched out and silently stacked arms before an equally silent Union army, for the Federal troops saw before them an army whose line was never broken.

The Confederacy's defeat at Gettysburg and at Vicksburg figuratively tore out its heart. Grant's Vicksburg campaign was the most brilliant single campaign of the war. By taking an inferior force, by abandoning his lines of communication, by using great speed, he had divided and conquered his enemy. Grant had gambled and won.

He had been severely criticized for two years but now recognition and acclaim were coming his way. A grateful nation considered him its leading general. And, seemingly, so did its President. Not recalling if they had ever met, Lincoln wrote him a letter of "grateful acknowledgment for the almost inestimable service" he had rendered the country. Frankly, he told him he thought Grant would "march the troops across the neck, run the batteries with the transports" but that Lincoln had no faith, only hope, that he would succeed. He concluded his letter: "I now wish to make personal acknowledgement that you were right, and I was wrong."

81

CONFEDERATE LIFE LINE—The key to the Mississippi River, which divided the Confederacy in two, was the city of Vicksburg. Grant, in his dispatch of March 20, 1863, stated: "In my opinion, the opening of the Mississippi River will be to us of more advantage than the capture of forty Richmonds." Vicksburg's batteries on the bluffs commanded five miles of the river. J. E. Taylor's painting depicts the running of the batteries by the Union fleet. Courtesy Library of Congress.

GALVANIZED CONFEDERATES—The commandant at Vicksburg was the able Pennsylvanian Lt. Gen. John C. Pemberton. Shown here is Maj. Gen. Martin Luther Smith. A New Yorker by birth, a professional soldier, an army engineer of great ability who had developed the defenses of Vicksburg; intelligent and of fine character, he commanded the Confederate left in this greatest of western objectives. Courtesy Library of Congress.

ADMIRAL DAVID DIXON PORTER—Porter was the second admiral of the United States Navy. He rendered distinguished service at Vicksburg. Courtesy Library of Congress.

ADMIRAL DAVID GLASGOW FARRAGUT—Farragut became the Navy's first vice admiral, December 23, 1864, and first admiral, July 25, 1866. He was responsible for opening up the lower Mississippi River early in the Civil War. Courtesy Library of Congress.

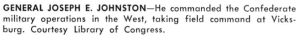

GENERAL JOSEPH E. JOHNSTON—He commanded the Confederate military operations in the West, taking field command at Vicksburg. Courtesy Library of Congress.

MAJOR GENERAL WILLIAM S. ROSECRANS—In July and August of 1863, Halleck urged Rosecrans to move against Bragg who had his headquarters at Chattanooga. Rosecrans did not move until August 16th. Engaging in the battle of Chicamauga where he was defeated on September 20th, he was forced into a position of siege at Chattanooga. He despised Grant. Courtesy Library of Congress.

VICKSBURG TRANSPORTS—Paddle-wheelers such as these were used to ferry troops and supplies across the Mississippi under the protective hands of Adm. David D. Porter. Photo by William Pywell. Courtesy Library of Congress.

POPULAR IDOL—This lithograph from a painting by Alonzo Chappel found a ready sale in 1863. Courtesy Detroit Historical Museum.

Chapter Nine

A New Chief For the North

A new Grant had emerged from Vicksburg—a totally different commander than at Belmont for there, and at Donelson and Shiloh, he had made serious mistakes. But he had not repeated them—for the Vicksburg campaign had been flawless.

Having been made a major general in the regular army as of July 4, 1863, made no difference in his outward appearance or actions. Modest, sincere, thoughtful, straightforward, pleasant, unpretentious, unemotional, he was usually deep in thought as he restlessly turned or chewed an unlighted cigar. Correspondent Frank B. Wilkie of the New York *Times* described him as "a small but compactly built man of about 45 years of age . . . (wearing) a plain blue suit, without scarf, sword or trappings of any sort, save the double-starred shoulder strap — an indifferently good 'Kossuth' hat, with the top battered in close to his head; full beard of a cross between 'light' and 'sandy'; a square cut face, whose lines and contour indicated endurance and determination, . . ."

After mopping up around Vicksburg, Grant visited General Nathanial P. Banks at New Orleans to discuss troop movements. The horse he was riding shied at a locomotive in the street, slipped and fell on him, seriously crushing his thigh and rendering him unconscious. Recovering sufficiently in a week, he was carried aboard a steamer and taken to Vicksburg where he remained with his family convalescing for over a month.

While he was under orders to proceed to Louisville, his train was boarded on October 17th at Indianapolis by Secretary of War Stanton. With the black-bearded, bespectacled Stanton was Ohio's Governor Brough, neither of whom had ever seen or met Grant. Stanton approached the rather distinguished appearing Dr. Edward Kittoe, Grant's staff surgeon, vigorously shook his hand and remarked: "How are you, General Grant? I knew you from your pictures."

The Confederate victory at Chickamauga on September 19 and 20 had given the South new hope. The Union army, now at Chattanooga under General William Stark Rosecrans, who otherwise was a competent officer but who had lost confidence in the defeat, was surrounded by General Braxton Bragg's army.

Stanton gave Grant orders placing him in command of the newly created Military Division of the Mississippi with permission to relieve Rosecrans if he wished. He did, assigning General George H. Thomas in his place. Grant arrived in Chatanooga October 23rd; by October 28th he had broken the Confederate lines sufficiently to establish a "Cracker Line"

SECRETARY OF WAR EDWIN McMASTERS STANTON—Grant and Stanton first met at Indianapolis on June 17, 1863. They journeyed to Louisville where Grant was given command of the Military Division of the Mississippi comprising the Departments of the Ohio, Cumberland, and Tennessee. Courtesy Library of Congress.

of supply to the besieged Union troops.

With the Army of the Cumberland under Thomas, the Army of the Tennessee under Sherman and a detachment of the Army of the Potomac under Major General Joseph Hooker, the battle for Chattanooga began with Thomas' demonstration November 23rd. That day Orchard Knob was taken, and on the 25th the impregnable Missionary Ridge was assaulted successfully, ending the seige and routing Bragg. With Bragg defeated and driven south, all of Tennessee came under Northern domination. The mountainous defense line was

pierced and possession of the Chattanooga railroad center opened a line of approach to Richmond via Knoxville that the Union controlled for the balance of the war.

This great victory brought additional recognition to Grant. The people of the North wanted him rewarded as did his backers, Elihu Washburne and Governor Yates. Though there were prominent politicians who had some doubts, they yielded to popular demand. A bill was introduced in Congress recreating the office of lieutenant general with the understanding Grant would receive the promotion. On February 26, 1864, it became a law, and on March 1st Lincoln submitted Grant's nomination, which was confirmed the following day.

When Grant was summoned to Washington to be made General-in-Chief, he wrote to Sherman: "What I want is to express my thanks to you and McPherson as the men to whom, above all others, I feel indebted for what ever I have had of success." Sherman immediately replied, denying that either he or General McPherson had given any great assistance—that he, Grant, had shown signs of greatness at Belmont when neither was near, and at Donelson when Sherman was not near and McPherson was too subordinate to influence him.

The 42-year-old Grant registered in at the Willard Hotel in Washington on March 8, 1864, his only companion and attendant being his 14-year-old son Fred. A reception in his honor at the White house that evening was one of the few occasions on which he wore his uniform vest and coat buttoned to the top. When he arrived, there was so much confusion in the large crowd present that he was asked to stand on a sofa so all could see him.

On the following day Lincoln presented him with his commission at the Executive Mansion in the presence of the Cabinet. In Grant's first interview with Lincoln, the President indicated he was not a military man and never wanted to interfere with them but, because of the procrastination of his commanders and the pressure of Congress and the people, he was forced to issue his series of military orders. He knew some were wrong and thought perhaps they all were. "All he wanted, or had ever wanted, was someone who would take the responsibility and act," wrote Grant.

He continued: "In one of my early interviews with the President I expressed my dissatisfaction with the little that had been accomplished by the cavalry so far in the war, and the belief that it was capable of accomplishing much more than it had done if under a thorough leader. I said I wanted the very best man in the army for that command. Halleck was present and spoke up, saying, 'How would Sheridan do?' I replied, 'The very man I want.' The President said I could have anyone I wanted."

Halleck served as Grant's Chief of Staff in Washington, acting as military advisor to Lincoln and Stanton. Sherman was given Grant's former command, and Major General George Gordon Meade continued in command of the Army of the Potomac. Now commanding 21 army corps consisting of 533,000 men, and a staff of 14 officers, Grant made his headquarters with the Army of the Potomac on March 10th near Brandy Station. He wrote to Sherman on April 4th: "It is my design, if the enemy keep quiet and allow me to take the initiative in the spring campaign, to work all parts of the army together, and somewhat toward a common center."

He considered his military problem to be quite simple. Capturing cities and large land areas was of little value, as long as an enemy army was free to move about. There were two such armies—Robert E. Lee's Army of Northern Virginia and Joseph E. Johnston's Army of Tennessee. Destroy these two armies as rapidly as possible and the fate of the South was sealed.

Sherman would handle the Western theater while he would take on Lee. Though the Army of the Potomac had adequate combat experience, it had had poor leadership. And constant interference from the War Department had its ill effect. Grant supplied a firm hand by remaining with it though he issued no orders except through Meade, permitting no outside interference whatsoever. His mission was to head for Richmond to destroy the army Lee would offer to defend it.

Grant did not have Lee's experience in fighting on Virginia terrain but he had a broader experience. His advantage over Lee was that of being able to direct operations outside of the Army of the Potomac; Lee was confined to directing only the Army of Northern Virginia.

When Grant's appointment was announced at Lee's headquarters, one of the officers present confidently voiced the ease with which they would whip the new general. General Longstreet, being present, said: "Do you know Grant? Well, I do. I was in the corps of cadets with him at West Point for three years. I was present at his wedding.

Battle of CHICAMAUGA—Painted by James Walker. Courtesy Library of Congress.

GENERAL JAMES LONGSTREET—Graduating a year ahead of Grant, he was present at Grant's wedding. He was at his best in battle. Though reliable as an executive officer, it still is argued that he failed Lee at Gettysburg. Courtesy Library of Congress.

I served in the same army with him in Mexico. I have observed his methods of warfare in the West, and I believe I know him through and through, and I tell you that we cannot afford to underrate him and the army he now commands."

In Grant's command, a general officer sounded off about knowing Lee's method from experience and how Lee would throw his entire army between them and the Rapidan and cut Union communications. Grant, with considerable feeling, said: "Oh, I am heartily tired of hearing about what Lee is going to do. Some of you always seem to think he is suddenly going to turn a double summersault, and land in our rear and on both of our flanks at the same time. Go back to your command, and try to think what we are going to do ourselves, instead of what Lee is going to do."

Colonel James Wilson once had heard Sherman say he knew he was much smarter than Grant and knew more than he did about tactics, strategy, history and everything else, "but Wilson, I'll tell you where he beats me and where he beats the world. He don't care a damn for what the enemy does out of his sight, but it scares me like hell."

Grant had ordered a simultaneous advance on all fronts—Sherman was to drive toward Atlanta, sweeping Joe Johnston's forces before him; Franz Sigel was to take the Valley of Virginia; Banks had Mobile as his objective, and Ben Butler was to get behind Lee south of the James River.

At the beginning of the campaign, Meade repeatedly either modified or changed Sheridan's orders, interfering with the over-all strategy and operations. In an altercation resulting from a dressing down Meade had given Sheridan for allegedly impeding the march of the Fifth Corps, Sheridan told him he could take the Confederate cavalry star Jeb Stuart's hide if permitted a free rein. The overwrought Meade repeated this to Grant, who replied: "Did Sheridan say that? Well, he generally knows what he is talking about. Let him start right out and do it."

Sheridan started out the next morning and defeated Stuart's cavalry, during which action Stuart was mortally wounded. Getting to the Confederate rear, Sheridan broke up the Virginia Central Railroad on May 9, 1864, and destroyed valuable supplies. Sheridan could not regard the South in any light but that of an enemy.

Lee, as usual, selected the position most suited to him. This battle of the Wilderness began at dawn of May 4th and continued for several days, with any Union advance being paid for with great loss of life. Grant operated on the premise that the North had unlimited manpower and industrial strength. A war of attrition was the only kind of solution. "Hammering" the enemy, as he called it, and "pounding," as Sherman called it, ultimately would lead to a clash with Lee where unlimited supplies of materials and men would prove decisive. Grant was a man who would not be stopped by heavy losses. He'd take a deep breath, light another cigar, then give another punch.

In a message to Halleck from Spottsylvania Courthouse on May 11th, Grant stated: "I . . . purpose to fight it out on this line, if it takes all summer." With the repulses of Lee as he neared Richmond, Grant became more restive, a characteristic of his when a strong enemy was on his front. An able general on other fields, it was not evident in the Wilderness.

The road to Richmond led past Cold Harbor.

The heavily defended positions of the Confederates led to losses of such severity, with no comparable gain, that Grant was labeled by the press as "Grant the butcher." The long campaign, from Rapidan to Petersburg had cost Grant almost 55,000 men and he had not defeated Lee in the entire campaign, yet the policy of attrition had worn Lee down to the extent that he did not again assume the offensive. Later, Grant wrote: "I have always regretted that the last assault at Cold Harbor was ever made."

The 8,000 pounds of powder exploding in the mine at Petersburg made a large crater but the battle was lost to the Confederates through lack of initiative and leadership of Union officers. The Union forces surrounded Petersburg, beginning a siege that June that lasted until the following April, 1865. Hammering away at them during those months wore down the Confederate forces and used up their supplies, but they managed to muster a force that repelled every Union assault.

Sherman had begun his tremendous campaign marching through Georgia that succeeded in bringing Atlanta to its knees that September. When Sherman received Grant's congratulatory telegram, he replied: "I have received your dispatch, and will communicate it to the troops in general orders . . . I have always felt that you would personally take more pleasure in my success than in your own, and I reciprocate the feeling in its fullest extent."

On September 12th, Grant wrote him: "I feel you have accomplished the most gigantic undertaking given to any general in this war, and with a skill and ability that will be acknowledged in history as unsurpassed, if not unequaled. It gives me as much pleasure to record this in your favor as it would in favor of any living man, myself included." Adam Badeau, who knew them intimately, wrote: "Both men meant what they said."

Grant had advised the Secretary of War on August 10th that he thought it would be a just reward to appoint Sherman a major general and W. S. Hancock and Sheridan brigadiers in the regular army, since all had earned advancement. Later, on November 23rd, he met with Lincoln and Stanton in Washington, recommending the mustering out of eight major generals and 33 brigadiers to make room for officers winning promotion in the field. Thoughtfully, he suggested that of many of these, "it might be advisable to notify, so as to give them the opportunity of resigning, if they elect to do so." Lincoln reminded him that some were close personal friends. This he knew but was convinced they were not good generals and that it was for the good of the service that they be replaced.

Other than the continuance of the siege of Petersburg, Sheridan spent the balance of the year in raiding the fertile Shenandoah Valley of Virginia, destroying crops that could be used to feed Lee's army. Grant wanted all property useful to the enemy destroyed. "It is desirable," he said "that nothing should be left to invite the enemy to return. . . ."

UNION ENTRENCHMENTS AT VICKSBURG—Courthouse in distance. Courtesy of The New York Historical Society, New York City.

BATTLE OF CHATTANOOGA, TENNESSEE—The battle between Confederate General Braxton Bragg and Grant's beseiged forces began on November 23, 1863 and ended on the 25th. This Currier and Ives print shows the assault on Missionary Ridge. Courtesy Nationwide Insurance.

CAPTURE OF LOOKOUT MOUNTAIN—From a drawing by J. F. Hillen, November 25, 1863. Courtesy New York Public Library, Prints Division.

GRANT AT BATTLE OF CHATTANOOGA—Prang & Co. Lithograph of a Thulstrup painting. Courtesy Library of Congress.

INSPECTION AND REFLECTION—Left to right: U. S. Grant, Gen. J. A. Rawlins (seated, with back against tree), General Webster behind him, Col. Clark B. Lagow leaning against tree, and Col. William S. Hillyer in right foreground. An orderly is seated by the path at the rear.

They inspect Lookout Mountain at the spot where Gen. Hooker's men had waved a flag of victory November 25, 1863, just a few days earlier. Grant with crumpled hat, plain blouse, trousers tucked into his boots, and a cigar, wears a sword and epaulets which are quite unusual for him. Brady photo, National Archives.

UNION ARMY TRANSPORTS ON THE TENNESSEE RIVER—Taken below Chattanooga, Tennessee. Courtesy Library of Congress.

MEET GENERAL GRANT—President and Mrs. Lincoln held a reception in the East Room of the White House at 8 P.M. on March 8, 1864. Grant with his staff members arrived at 9.30 P.M., Lincoln and the crowd moving forward to meet him. They greeted each other cordially for this was their first meeting. This painting attributed to Francis B. Carpenter, is in the White House Collection.

ABRAHAM LINCOLN—This Brady photograph was used in preparing the engraved likeness of Lincoln on the Five Dollar Bill. Robert Lincoln thought this the 'best likeness of his father.' February 9, 1864. Courtesy Library of Congress.

GRANT RECEIVING HIS COMMISSION OF LIEUTENANT GEN-ERAL—Grant was the first man since George Washington to be accorded the full rank of Lieutenant General. The presentation was made on March 9th at 1 P.M. in the Cabinet Chambers by President Lincoln. An illustration in **Harper's Weekly**, March 20, 1864, courtesy Lincoln National Life Foundation.

MAJOR GENERAL GEORGE G. MEADE—When Grant was ap-pointed General-in-Chief, Meade, commanding the Army of the Potomac, pledged his complete support. Grant, to save Meade any embarrassment, gave all orders for movements of the Army of the Potomac to Meade. Meade was an intellectual with a well-disciplined engineer's mind. He was impatient and almost unapproachable in battle though very brave. Courtesy Library of Congress.

GENERAL JOE HOOKER—A fighting general, an able administra-tor, he was boastful and vain, caring little for the rights of others. It was at Chancellorsville he commanded 97,000 men and was decisively defeated by 57,000 men under Lee and Jackson. Courtesy Library of Congress.

YOU ARE VIGILANT AND SELF-RELIANT—Lincoln evidences his complete faith in Grant. Courtesy Missouri Historical Society.

THE PRESIDENT AND GENERALS OF THE CONFEDERATE STATES—Courtesy Library of Congress.

COMMANDER-IN-CHIEF AND HIS STAFF—Courtesy National Archives.

CONFEDERATE GENERAL AMBROSE POWELL HILL—Often displaying initiative and sound judgment when on his own, he lacked decision when in the vicinity of General Lee. Courtesy Library of Congress.

GENERAL AMBROSE BURNSIDE—This manly six-footer was well-educated, energetic, humble. At Lincoln's order, he replaced McClellan in November of 1862. After his defeat at Fredericksburg he was replaced by Joe Hooker. Courtesy Library of Congress.

GENERAL HENRY J. HUNT—Serving with the Army of the Potomac he was in command of the artillery in the battle of the Wilderness. Courtesy Library of Congress.

WHITTLING AND THINKING—Gen. Grant in the afternoon of the first day's fight at the Wilderness, May 7, 1864. Grant frequently whittled to aid his thinking processes but was never known to make anything other than chips. Pencil sketch by Charles W. Reed. Courtesy Library of Congress.

GENERAL CUSTER AND STAFF—This sketch by Alfred R. Waud apparently made in March, 1864 shows Custer and his men with their Confederate prisoners during the movement across the Rapidan River, Virginia. Courtesy Library of Congress.

HEADQUARTERS IN THE FIELD—This painting by Charles Stanley Reinhart shows Grant during the Wilderness campaign. It is unlikely he carried a saber. From Horace Porter's "Campaigning With Grant."

THE GRANT FAMILY—About 1864. Left to right: Ellen (Nellie), Ulysses, Jesse, Fred, Julia, and Ulysses, Jr. Courtesy Illinois State Historical Library.

SENDING A TELEGRAM—It appears that Alfred Waud was the one to sketch Grant telegraphing the news of the crossing of the Rapidan River in May, 1864. Courtesy Library of Congress.

CROSSING OF THE RAPIDAN AT GERMANNA FORD—On May 4, 1864 at dawn, Grant's Army of the Potomac began its advance into the Wilderness where Lee's forces were waiting. He had instructed Meade to go wherever Lee went. Here Grant is using pontoon bridges in this great advance. Courtsey Library of Congress.

WHEN GRANT TOOK CHARGE—Previously, all armies were independent. Grant planned to move all armies at once engaging the enemy on all fronts simultaneously. The Army of the James would be the left wing; the Army of the Potomac would take the center; the troops under Sherman would be the right wing. This drawing by Edwin Forbes was made on May 7, 1864, of the 6th Corps (Union) fighting in the Wilderness campaign. Courtesy library of Congress.

ON THE ROAD TO SPOTSYLVANIA COURT HOUSE, VA.—May 7, 1864. Grant received an ovation from his men as they passed him and his staff on their way from the Wilderness to Spotsylvania Court House. Pencil sketch by Edwin Forbes. Courtesy Library of Congress.

CENTER OF THE UNION POSITION AT SPOTSYLVANIA COURT HOUSE—Grant had placed himself with the Army of the Potomac, where the greatest opposition was expected. Pencil sketch May 9, 1864, by Edwin Forbes. Courtesy Library of Congress.

LEE CHECKMATES GRANT—In the latter part of May 1864, Grant's forces crossed the North Anna River on this pontoon bridge at Jericho Mill without opposition from Lee. Lee had folded in his flanks, permitting Grant's forces to cross on each side, splitting the Federal army. **Courtesy Library of Congress.**

GRANT DECIDES TO FIGHT—Grant, at the lower left, leans over the shoulder of General Meade to study a map held by him. Surrounding them and seated on pews taken from Bethesda Church next door are the members of their staffs waiting for him to decide whether "to crush Lee's army on the north side of the James . . . or to move the Union army south of the James without giving battle . . . to the vicinity of Petersburg." It is June 2, 1894. His decision resulted in the battle of Cold Harbor. Courtesy Library of Congress.

WAR HORSE "CINCINNATI"—General Grant with one of his favorite mounts at Cold Harbor, Va., June 4, 1864. Saddle blanket indicates he is a Major General though his shoulder boards indicate a three-star rank. Courtesy Library of Congress.

GRANT'S TROOPS AT CHARLES CITY COURT HOUSE—June 13, 1864. Courtesy Library of Congress.

GRANT WATCHING HIS ARMY CROSS THE JAMES RIVER—June 14, 1864. Using pontoon bridges he headed for Petersburg to begin an assault the following day. From Horace Porter's "Campaigning With Grant" drawn by B. W. Clinedinst.

MAP READING—Grant with Col. Rawlins seated by his side, at the Cold Harbor, Va. Headquarters on June 14, 1864. Grant studied maps continually, remembering every detail. From a stereo, courtesy of the Chicago Historical Society.

GENERAL HANCOCK'S CORPS CROSS THE JAMES RIVER—With a cigar in his mouth and sitting sidesaddle Grant watches just in back of Major General Hancock, who rests comfortably on his camp stool. This scene was drawn by William Waud on June 14, 1864, at Wilcox's Landing. Courtesy of Library of Congress.

GRANT LIKED FRESH MEAT BUT WELL DONE—While not living off the country a herd of beef was taken along and butchered as needed. A William Waud sketch in Harper's Weekly. Courtesy of Library of Congress.

PONTOON BRIDGE ON THE APPOMATTOX RIVER—Butler's headquarters below Petersburg, June, 1864. Drawing by Alfred R. Waud, courtesy Library of Congress.

PRISONERS OF WAR—They had survived the battle of Petersburg. Would they be as fortunate in surviving the illnesses common to all camp life or, best of all, would they be exchanged? Undoubtedly Lincoln and Grant thought of these things as the Confederates marched by. B. W. Clinedinst illustration in Porter's "Campaigning With Grant."

Chapter Ten

The End Came Quick

City Point, Virginia, had been chosen by Grant for his headquarters in June of 1864. He selected a level piece of ground on a high bluff overlooking the junction of the Appomattox and James Rivers. A log cabin was constructed for him on the lawn of a comfortable house that had been assigned to the Chief Quartermaster. Grant's cabin was divided by a board partition, making two rooms of it. On the plank flooring of one room was placed a camp bed and washstand. In the other were several wooden chairs and a table for maps and writing materials.

Prior to the building of the log cabin he had occupied a hospital tent as his office while a smaller connecting tent in the rear was used for sleeping purposes. His headquarters tent was in the middle of a line of tents about one hundred feet back from the edge of the bluff. A hospital tent fly was stretched in front of his office to make a shaded area in which he could work with his staff, and it was here most of his official interviews were held. Matters of greater secrecy required retiring to the office tent. A wooden staircase had been built to reach from headquarters down to the boat landing at the foot of the bluff.

In January of 1865, several peace commissioners from the Confederacy were conducted to Grant's headquarters. Alexander H. Stephens, Vice President of the Confederacy, Judge J. A. Campbell, Assistant Secretary of War, and R. M. T. Hunter, President *pro tempore* of the Confederate Senate, were given quarters aboard the steamer *Mary Martin* for several days to await the arrival of President Lincoln. During their stay Grant maintained a pleasant relationship but avoided any conversation relative to their mission.

He received a message on February 2nd directing them to Hampton Roads to meet the President and a member of his Cabinet. The meeting came to naught. Lincoln refused to negotiate unless they would concede that the Union must be preserved and slavery abolished. With these concessions he would have been willing to grant almost any terms.

Lincoln was a frequent visitor to City Point, seeming to relax away from the pressures of Washington. He watched the preparations for the spring offensive with great interest. During one of these visits he mentioned that his oldest son Robert, just graduated from Harvard, had requested permission to enter the military service and that he had granted permission with the *proviso* that he serve as a volunteer aide without pay or emoluments. Grant recommended he be given a commission and he would place him on his staff. Given the rank of captain, he joined the staff on February 23rd. Working hard and expecting no special treatment, he became quite popular with the other staff members.

The Honorable Elihu B. Washburne visited Grant at City Point on March 11th, presenting him with a gold medal ordered struck by Congress in recognition of his services to his country.

With the stalemate at Petersburg and the announcement of Sherman's march to Savannah, the press insisted that Grant was losing ground with the administration. This was made apparent with the introduction of a bill to make Sherman a lieutenant general. Sherman, on hearing of it, wrote his brother Senator John Sherman of Ohio, to stop it at once. To Grant he wrote: "I should emphatically decline any command calculated to bring us into rivalry."

From City Point on February 7th, Grant replied to him: "I have received your very kind letters in which you say you would decline, or are opposed to promotion. No one would be more pleased at your advancement than I, and if you should be placed in my position, and I subordinate, it should not change our relations in the least. I would make the same exertions to support you that you have ever done to support me, and would do all in my power to make our cause win."

Both knew that Sherman's march through Georgia, though worrying everyone in Washington, was carrying war to the heart of an empty shell. Lincoln had indicated that Grant was holding the leg while Sherman took off the skin. Grant's grip on Lee had been so tight Sherman was able to make his devastating move through Georgia practically unopposed.

Lincoln's last visit to City Point occurred March 24, 1865. Arriving on the *River Queen* with Mrs. Lincoln and their youngest son, Tad, they left March 29th. On the 28th he met in his cabin with Grant, Admiral Porter and Sherman to discuss strategy. He had made it a point to advise Grant and Sherman that he wanted no more bloodshed— just submission with the most liberal and honorable terms. There was no bitterness in him for he wanted no one punished. Grant asked: "Mr. President, did you at any time doubt the final success of the cause?" Lincoln replied, earnestly, "Never, for a moment."

There is no question that Sheridan's victory at

GENERAL GRANT AND STAFF AT CITY POINT, VA., JUNE, 1864—Standing, left to right: Capt. Henry W. Janes, quartermaster for headquarters; Gen. Grant; Major Michael Morgan, chief of commissary; Capt. Peter Hudson, aide-de-camp. Sitting, left to right: Col. John A. Rawlins without beard and mustache, assistant adjutant general and chief of staff; Col. Cyrus B. Comstock, aide-de-camp; Lt. Fred Grant, aide-de-camp; Col. Orville E. Babcock, aide-de-camp; Col. Ely S. Parker, military secretary (grandnephew of Seneca Chief Red Jacket, Six Nations). Brady photo, Library of Congress.

RELAXATION AT HEADQUARTERS, CITY POINT, VA.—June, 1864. Grant, third from left is attired in summer clothes. The staff members are equally unconventional in their dress. Having lost nearly 50,000 men in the three successive battles of Cold Harbor, Spotsylvania, and the Wilderness, he appears undaunted. Brady photo, Library of Congress.

Five Forks on April 1, 1865, was the beginning of the end, and forced Lee to abandon Petersburg and Richmond two days later. With word of Sheridan's victory, Grant's battle instinct was aroused. Sensing what Lee would do, he ordered an immediate assault along the entire front to prevent any concentration on Sheridan, who was well in the advance. Sheridan's battle report of April 6th concluded: "If the thing is pressed, I think that Lee will surrender." Grant forwarded the dispatch to Lincoln, receiving the reply: "Let the thing be pressed."

In the afternoon of April 7th, Grant wrote Lee a note from the Farmville Hotel where Lee had slept just the night before: "The result of the last week must convince you of the hopelessness of further resistance of the Army of Northern Virginia . . . and regard it as my duty to shift from myself the responsibility of any further effusion of blood, by asking of you . . . to surrender . . ."

At this point, some of Lee's officers had suggested surrender, but he denied them their request by replying to Grant "I have received your note this day. Though not entirely of the opinion you express of the hopelessness of further resistance . . . I reciprocate your desire to avoid useless effusion of blood, and therefore . . . ask the terms you will offer on condition of its surrender."

Receiving this note early on the morning of

April 8th, Grant immediately replied: "In reply I would say that, peace being my great desire, there is but one condition that I would insist upon, namely, that the men and officers surrendered shall be disqualified for taking up arms against the government of the United States until properly exchanged."

The Union troops continued to push, Grant saying to Sheridan, "I think Lee will surrender today." By dusk General George Armstrong Custer had captured four heavily loaded trains of supplies, one of which was burned, the other three being manned and sent toward Farmville. Pushing toward Appomattox Courthouse, Custer captured 25 pieces of artillery, a hospital train and numerous prisoners.

At midnight Grant received a message from Lee indicating he did "not think the emergency had arisen to call for the surrender of this army." At the moment of writing he did not know what Custer had done to him. Earlier that day Sheridan had indicated to Grant: "If it is possible to push on your troops we may have handsome results in the morning." And later, "I do not think Lee means to surrender unless compelled to do so."

Grant's response to Lee's suggestion to discuss peace was: "I have no authority to treat on the subject of peace . . . (Stanton previously rebuked Grant for considering any negotiations with the enemy but for the purpose of surrender). The

112

NO SECRET PLANS AT HEADQUARTERS—When Grant's staff met at City Point, Va. in June, 1864, under the open tent fly, plans discussed were in generalities. Secrecy was maintained by going into the wall tent. Seated, left to right: Gen. Grant, Gen. Rawlins, Lt. Col. W. L. Duff, Lt. Col. Horace Porter, Capt. Ely Parker; standing, left to right: Lt. Col. Adam Badeau, Lt. Col. C. B. Comstock (engineer), Lt. Col. Fred Dent, Lt. Col. O. E. Babcock, last officer unidentified. Courtesy Chicago Historical Society.

terms upon which peace can be had are well understood. . . ."

Lee responded by approaching the Union cavalry. Sheridan directed his cavalry to fall back slowly and with resistance, giving Ord time to form his lines and attack. Lee's infantry greatly outnumbered Sheridan's dismounted troops. Crook and his men soon were in the thick of it for he was engaged on his front. With heavy resistance on their front, the rapidly advancing Confederates came to a halt, and then began to fall back. Three Union infantry commands moved forward in double quick time as Sheridan prepared to flank the enemy. Suddenly Lee sent forward a white flag. Assur-

CITY POINT WHARF—By early June, 1864, the army of the Potomac was using City Point, Va., as a base of supplies. Courtesy Library of Congress.

SUMMER OF 1864 AT CITY POINT, VA.—Grant and his staff of faithful followers. Neither expressing himself or showing any emotion he would listen carefully to all ideas expressed then decide upon a course of action that would never be made known in advance. Courtesy Library of Congress.

ances were given that negotiations were in process, a circumstance about which there is some argument.

Lee had sent Grant a note which he received at 11:50 a.m. of the 9th, stating: "I now ask an interview, in accordance with the offer contained in your letter of yesterday . . . with reference to the surrender of this army. . . ."

Grant, who had been suffering with a severe sick headache, felt it instantly leave. Lee, who had been nursing his rheumatism, was not so fortunate. Grant replied to Lee's message by suggesting that he select a place for the conference. Sheridan could hardly contain himself, for his experience had convinced him the flag of truce was but a trick. Meeting Adam Badeau he said: "I've got 'em," as he doubled up his fist, "I've got 'em, like that."

Wilmer McLean's farmhouse was the site selected by Lee for the important meeting. He arrived there to meet Grant at the threshold. Elaborately dressed in a new uniform, embroidered gauntlets, burnished sword and all, Lee attributed this to Sheridan's raid on his headquarters train a few days before in which he saved but one suit of clothes.

In contrast, Grant was swordless, wearing a worn and soiled uniform and muddy boots. He had been too busy to clean up.

Following a few preliminary remarks of their days during the Mexican campaign, they turned to the business at hand. Grant felt sorry for Lee, who had fought so valiantly and lost. His wish was to spare the feelings of this great opponent. As Lee later said: "No man could have behaved better than Grant did under the circumstances. He did not touch my sword; the usual custom is for the sword to be received when tendered, and then handed back, but he did not touch mine."

Grant asked his staff secretary for writing materials, then began to draft the terms of surrender. All weapons and supplies must be given up, and all men paroled. Officers could keep their sidearms, private horses and baggage. All officers and men would be allowed to return to their homes and would not be disturbed by United States authorities as long as they obeyed the laws and observed their paroles.

Lee considered the terms magnanimous and as having a good effect upon the men. After writing a letter of acceptance of the terms offered, and signing it, Lee indicated his army was without food or forage. Grant promptly provided him with rations for 25,000 men from the train captured by Custer.

The news of the signing started the firing of salutes. Grant ordered it stopped at once, saying: "The war is over; the rebels are our countrymen

114

THE SHENANDOAH FOR SHERIDAN—It was Grant's plan to place Sheridan in the Shenandoah Valley to become the center of the Union line. There he was to lay waste the Confederates' supplies and destroy the troops that gathered them. Drawing from Maryland Heights in 1864, by Alfred R. Waud. Courtesy Library of Congress.

again, and the best sign of rejoicing after the victory will be to abstain from all demonstrations in the field."

The following morning Grant and Lee met for a half hour discussing means of restoring peace and harmony. Lee then left for Richmond and, at noon, Grant left for City Point on a special train that left the hastily constructed track three times en route.

Grant reached Washington April 13, and again stayed at the Willard Hotel. He was invited by the President to meet with the Cabinet in the forenoon of the next day, Friday. This meeting was a cordial one in which they discussed means of bringing hostilities to a rapid close. Both the President and Mrs. Lincoln invited him to attend

the last performance of Miss Laura Keene in *Our American Cousin* at Ford's Theatre that evening. Grant declined the invitation as he and Mrs. Grant had made plans to visit their children at Burlington, New Jersey. And with the President's mention of a demonstration in his honor at the theater, Grant became even less inclined. A note at that point from Mrs. Grant expressing her desire to leave on the 4 o'clock train was final. At 2 o'clock he shook Lincoln's hand and bid him goodbye.

Near midnight in Philadelphia, while eating lunch at Bloodgood's Hotel near the Delaware River ferry, he was handed a telegram. After receiving two more he told Mrs. Grant of the assassination and the warning to look out for his own safety.

PETERSBURG MINE EXPLOSION—This huge mine was exploded by the Federals on July 30, 1864. The poorly executed assault that followed ended in failure. Grant knew that the end was near for "the rebels have now in their ranks their last man. . . . A man lost by them cannot be replaced." Drawing by A. R. Waud. Courtesy Library of Congress.

Joe Johnston was getting ready to surrender in North Carolina. Sherman had been negotiating a peace with him, the results of which were entirely unacceptable to President Johnson and Secretary Stanton. Grant hurried down to Raleigh on April 24th, to inform Sherman delicately of Johnson's disapproval and suggest that he offer the same terms agreed upon by Lee. On April 26th Johnston and Sherman agreed upon terms identical to those Lee had accepted. The Civil War was over.

Immediately, Stanton published a paper denouncing Sherman as a traitor who had sold himself to Confederate leaders. Grant had kept in the background while Sherman had met with Johnston, but he had endorsed the new terms of surrender. Stanton's scathing rebuke of Sherman caused Grant to protest.

By June, President Johnson and others took steps to indict Lee and other Confederate officers for treason. Grant protested to the President in writing, and finally in person. When Johnson would not comply, Grant declared he would resign his commission if the paroles he had issued were violated. With this conclusion from Grant, the proceedings were abandoned.

SHERIDAN'S RIDE AT THE BATTLE OF CEDAR CREEK—Returning from Washington on October 19, 1864, to find a good share of his troops retreating and demoralized, he dashed toward the front rallying his men as he went. His inspired men responded by presenting him with a victory. A. R. Waud drawing, courtesy Library of Congress.

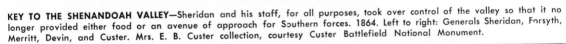

SHERIDAN'S WAGON TRAIN—In his campaign in the Shenandoah Valley during the summer of 1864 Sheridan destroyed such stock and crops as he could not carry off. Courtesy Library of Congress.

KEY TO THE SHENANDOAH VALLEY—Sheridan and his staff, for all purposes, took over control of the valley so that it no longer provided either food or an avenue of approach for Southern forces. 1864. Left to right: Generals Sheridan, Forsyth, Merritt, Devin, and Custer. Mrs. E. B. Custer collection, courtesy Custer Battlefield National Monument.

LIEUTENANT GENERAL GRANT AT CITY POINT—This was Brady's last photograph of Grant in the field. August 1864.
Courtesy Library of Congress.

GENERAL J. E. B. STUART, C.S.A.— As chief of the Confederate cavalry he lived on praise and earned it by refusing to admit defeat. Though a master of reconnaissance and lightning attack he was absent when Lee needed him most—at Gettysburg. Courtesy Library of Congress.

SHERIDAN'S FINAL CHARGE AT WINCHESTER—When Sheridan led a charge his men followed. Lithograph by Prang & Co. Courtesy Library of Congress.

IN THE WAKE OF THE CAVALRY—
A. R. Waud draws a scene showing the Third Cavalry Division commanded by General Custer retiring from burning forage near Mt. Jackson, October 7, 1864. Courtesy Library of Congress.

BRIG. GEN. ALFRED T. A. TORBERT AND CAVALRY STAFF—Torbert was appointed Chief of Cavalry, Army of the Shenandoah in August, 1864, by Sheridan. Torbert, in the center with his saber resting on its point, was most effective in the valley operations in September and October, 1864. Courtesy Library of Congress.

DISDAIN FOR BURSTING SHELLS— Grant's apparent unconcern stems from his deep concentration on the importance of a message that could win a battle or save many lives. From Horace Porter's "Campaigning With Grant."

WINTER QUARTERS AT CITY POINT, VA.—Grant's headquarters from June 4, 1864 until the surrender of Lee, it was on an elevated bluff at the junction of the Appomattox and James rivers. Grant and his staff first lived in tents, building the more substantial cabins for winter use. The cabin constructed with vertical logs was Grant's. B. W. Clinedinst illustration in Porter's "Campaigning With Grant."

NEARING THE END—Brig. Gen. John Rawlins, Lieut. Gen. Grant, and Col. T. S. Bowers, (from left to right) meet in front of City Point, Va. headquarters during the winter of 1864-1865. Brady photo, courtesy Library of Congress.

WATERFRONT FACILITIES AT CITY POINT—Military supplies at the James River docks. Brady photo, National Archives. Courtesy Ansco Historical Collections.

THOSE WHO ASSISTED SHERIDAN
—Left to right: Generals Wesley Merritt, David McM. Gregg, Philip Henry Sheridan, Henry E. Davies, James Harrison Wilson, and Alfred T. A. Torbert. In 1865, Wilson commanded the cavalry corps in the Mississippi military district; Torbert commanded the cavalry corps of the Army of the Shenandoah under Sheridan. Courtesy Library of Congress.

CITY POINT RAILROAD—Grant used rail transporation for moving supplies in the rear of his lines finding it the only reliable means of competing with the mud. Courtesy Library of Congress.

A GENERAL'S HORSE—During the Civil War a horse was his best friend. There was no better means of conveyance over rough terrain. This horse of Grant's is thought to be "Egypt." Brady photo, courtesy National Archives.

THE OLD GRIMSLEY SADDLE AND BRIDLE—These were Grant's favorites during the campaigns of 1864 and 1865. Courtesy Chicago Historical Society Museum.

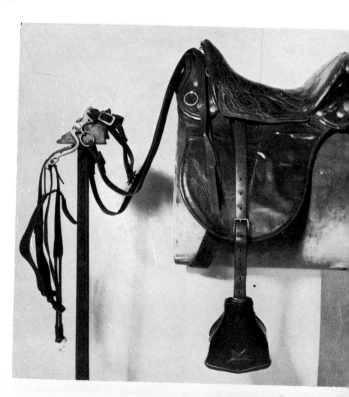

ALEXANDER H. STEPHENS—As Vice President of the Confederacy, he, with Judge Campbell, Assistant Secretary of War, and R. M. T. Hunter, a member of the Confederate Senate, visited Grant at the end of January, 1865, as peace commissioners. Grant was directed to send them to Hampton Roads for an interview. Courtesy Library of Congress.

THE PEACEMAKERS—Left to right: General Sherman, General Grant, President Lincoln and Admiral Porter. This conference was held at City Point on board the steamer **River Queen**, March 27-28, 1865. (Lincoln "wanted peace on almost any terms.") Painted by G. P. A. Healy. Courtesy The White House Collection.

R. M. T. Hunter—Formerly a U.S. Senator, he and the other peace commissioners met with Lincoln about February 2nd. They were unwilling to agree that the Union must be preserved and that slavery be abolished. Courtesy Library of Congress.

FAMILY MAN AT WAR—Grant with his wife and son Jesse in front of their cabin at City Point, Va. early in 1865. Mrs. Grant and her boys frequently stayed with the General when circumstances permitted. Courtesy Library of Congress.

SURROUNDED BY STAFF MEMBERS AT CITY POINT, VA. IN MARCH, 1865—Nearly all of these men were present when Lee signed the surrender one month later. Left to right: Col. Horace Porter, Col. William Duff, Col. T. S. Bowers, Col. J. D. Webster, Gen. John G. Barnard, Gen. John A. Rawlins, Gen. U. S. Grant, Gen. M. R. Patrick, Gen. Seth Williams, Gen. Rufus Ingalls, Col. Adam Badeau, Col. E. S. Parker; three men standing at extreme right end and seated figure not identified. Brady photo, Courtesy National Archives.

SHERIDAN'S CHARGE AT FIVE FORKS, VA.—Sheridan's victory on April 1st at Five Forks forced Lee to abandon Richmond two days later. From a painting by A. C. Redwood, courtesy Library of Congress.

LIEUTENANT GENERAL WADE HAMPTON, C.S.A.—This South Carolinian was one of the richest men in the South at the beginning of the war. Using a million dollars of his own money to equip a cavalry force he ended the war penniless and without a home to live in. An unconquerable spirit, he did not ask the impossible. Courtesy Library of Congress.

GENERAL JUBAL ANDERSON EARLY, C.S.A.—Though prejudiced against cavalry he believed that Lee consistently and seriously under-estimated the size of Sheridan's forces in the Shenandoah Valley. Courtesy Library of Congress.

CUMP SHERMAN—Two years older than Grant, thin, tall and sharp-featured, his speech was rapid, erupting from a mind crowded with ideas. He thought in terms of geographical objectives while Grant thought in terms of the enemy's army as his chief objective. Courtesy Library of Congress.

A GRATEFUL PRESIDENT—Lincoln and Grant were prepared for what they knew would happen any day. At the right is Lincoln's son Tad and Admiral Porter. The meeting took place in Petersburg on April 4. Painted by B. W. Clinedinst for Porter's "Campaigning With Grant."

LIEUTENANT GENERAL U. S. GRANT—Wearing black crepe on his left arm in mourning for the death of his Commander-in-Chief Abraham Lincoln. Photo by F. Gutekunst, Philadelphia, in late 1865. Courtesy Chicago Historical Society.

Head Quarters Armies of the United States,
City Point, April 7. 11 A.M. 1865

Lieut Gen. Grant.

Gen. Sheridan says "If the thing
is pressed I think that Lee will surrender." Let
the thing be pressed.

A. Lincoln

This original dispatch sent by
Mr. Lincoln to me, Apl. 7ᵗʰ 1865,
U. S. Grant

LET THE THING BE PRESSED—So said President Lincoln to General Grant on April 7, 1865. Courtesy Chicago Historical Society.

SCENE OF THE GRANT AND LEE MEETING AT APPOMATTOX COURT HOUSE, VA.—The surrender terms were composed by Grant and accepted by Lee in the room to the left of the doorway of the McLean House shown here, April 9, 1865. Courtesy Library of Congress.

SURRENDER TERMS—Grant's term Lee considered magnani-mous and did much to dissipate the bitterness of defeat. Courtesy National Park Service.

THE LEE SURRENDER TABLE—Table on which it is alleged that General Lee wrote and signed his letter accepting Grant's surrender terms. Courtesy Chicago Historical Society whose museum possesses the marble-topped table.

DETROIT REJOICES WITH THE NATION—The Campus Martius is a small park in the business center of Detroit. This broadside courtesy of Burton Historical Collections, Detroit Public Library.

SURRENDER OF GEN. LEE!

"The Year of Jubilee has come!   Let all the People Rejoice!"

200 GUNS WILL BE FIRED

On the Campus Martius,

AT 3 O'CLOCK TO-DAY, APRIL 10,

To Celebrate the Victories of our Armies.   1865

Every Man, Woman and Child is hereby ordered to be on hand prepared to Sing and Rejoice. The crowd are expected to join in singing Patriotic Songs.

ALL PLACES OF BUSINESS MUST BE CLOSED AT 2 O'CLOCK.

Hurrah for Grant and his noble Army.

By Order of the People.

PEACE IN UNION—Grant and Lee at Appomattox. Painted by Thomas Nast and displayed in the Galena Historical Museum. Courtesy Galena Historical Society.

SURRENDER OF LEE AND GRANT—Painted by L. M. D. Guillame. Courtesy Appomattox Court House National Historical Park.

SURRENDER AT APPOMATTOX—There is considerable controversy as to which table served the two principals. Col. Charles Marshall, Lee's military secretary, assists with: "Col. Parker (Grant's military secretary) then took the little table back to the corner of the room, and made a copy of the terms in ink. I then took my seat at that table, and wrote Gen. Lee's reply to Gen. Grant. The table was then carried back by Col. Parker and placed by Gen. Grant's side with the ink copy which he signed. I laid the draft of Gen. Lee's copy on the marble-topped table, and he signed it." Lithograph by Major & Knapp, 1867.

GRANT AT APPOMATTOX—The surrender scene in the McLean farm house as Col. Horace Porter recalled it. Painted by B. W. Clinedinst for Horace Porter's "Campaigning With Grant."

THE GRANT SURRENDER TABLE—This table was used by Grant to draft the terms of surrender. Sheridan purchased it from Mr. McLean and presented it to General Custer's wife Libbie. Photo by J. G. Hill of Monroe.

GRANT AT APPOMATTOX.

THE DAY AFTER THE SURRENDER—On April 10th at 9 A.M., Grant rode out to a mound in the valley between the two armies where Lee came out to meet him. Out of earshot of their staffs they discussed means of restoring peace and harmony for nearly an hour. Painted by Otto Botticher, 1866. Courtesy Col. Brice C. W. Custer.

AFTER THE SURRENDER—General Lee and his aide leaving the McLean house at Appomattox Court House, April 9, 1865. There were no photographers to record the surrender. Drawing probably by Alfred R. Waud. Courtesy Library of Congress.

NEW BROOM—While the nation was genuinely sorrowful over the tragic loss of Lincoln the Radicals looked upon Vice President Andrew Johnson as a godsend. Johnson maintained that treason was a crime that merited punishment. The same Radical Senators that lapped up this form of speech were among those who attempted to impeach him three years later.

TROPHY COLLECTORS—Alfred R. Waud sketches soldiers cutting up the tree under which, it was rumored, Grant and Lee met. Actually, they did not meet until Lee greeted him on the porch of the McLean house. More than likely this is the apple tree under which Lee last sat just before riding to the McLean house. Courtesy Library of Congress.

GRANT NOTIFIES SECRETARY STANTON—A meager message it is true, but like all of Grant's—to the point. Courtesy National Archives.

HAPPY DAY IN ILLINOIS—Courtesy Chicago Historical Society.

NEW HOPE FOR THE FUTURE—Exchange of correspondence between Grant and Lee. Courtesy St. Louis Public Library.

DAILY PRESS
EXTRA.

PEACE!

SURRENDR OF GENERAL LEE.

ALL MUNITIONS OF WAR

ARTILLERY AND PUBLIC PROPERTY SURREND-ERED TO GRANT.

LEE'S OFFICERS AND MEN PAROLED

WAR DEPARTMENT,
WASHINGTON, April 9—9 P. M.

To Major General POPE, Commanding:

The Department has just received the official report of the surrender this day of Lee and his army to Lieut. Gen. Grant on the terms proposed by Gen. Grant. Details will be given as speedily as possible.

(Signed) E. M. STANTON,
Secretary of War.

HEADQ'RS ARMY OF THE UNITED STATES,
4 P. M., April 9 1865.

To Hon. E. M. Stanton, Secretary of War:

Gen. Lee surrendered the army of Northern Virginia this afternoon, upon terms proposed by myself. The accompanying and the additional correspondence will show the conditions fully. (Signed,)
U. S. GRANT, Lieutenant General.

APRIL 9th, 1865.

General: I received your note of this morning on the picket line, whither I have come to meet you and ascertain definitely what terms were embraced in your propositions of yesterday with reference to the surrender of this army. I now request an interview in accordance with offer contained in your letter of yesterday for that purpose.

Very respectfully,
Your obedient servant,
[Signed] R. E. LEE, General.

To Lieut. Gen. U. S. GRANT, commading armies of the United States.

APRIL 9, 1865.

To Gen. R. E. LEE, Commanding Armies Confederate States of America.

Your note this day is this moment received—11:15 A. M. In consequence of my having passed from the Richmond and Lynchburg road to the Farmville road, I am at this writing about four miles west of Walter's Church, and will push forward to the front for the purpose of meeting you. A notice, if sent to me on this road, when you wish the interview to take place, will meet me.

Very respectfully, your obedient servant,
U. S. GRANT,
Lieutenant General.

APPOMATTOX C. H., April 9th, 1865.

To Gen. R. E. LEE, Commanding C. S. A.:

In accordance with the substance of my letter to you of the 8th inst., I propose to receive the surrender of the Army of Northern Virginia on the following terms, viz:

Rolls of all the officers and men to be made in duplicate, one copy to be given to an officer designated by me; the other to be retained by such officer or officers as you may designate. The officers to give their individual paroles not to take up arms against the Government of the United States until properly exchanged, and each company or regiment commander sign a like parole for the men in their command. The arms, artillery and public property to be parked or stacked and turned over to officers appointed by me to receive them. This will not embrace the side arms of officers nor their private horses or baggage.

This done each officer and man will be allowed to return to their homes not to be disturbed by the United States authorities so long as they observe the parole and the laws in force where they may reside.

Very respectfully,
U. S. GRANT, Lieut. Gen.

HDQR'S, ARMY NORTHERN VIRGINIA,
April 9th.

To Lieut-Gen. U. S. Grant, commanding U. S. Armies:

I have received your letter of this date containing the terms of surrender of the army of Northern Virginia as proposed by you. As they are substantially the same as those expressed in your letter of the 8th inst., they are accepted. I will proceed to designate the proper officer to carry the stipulations into effect.

Very respectfully your obedient servant.
R. E. LEE, General.

The following is the previous correspondence between Lieut. Gen. Grant and Gen. Lee referred to in the foregoing telegrams:

CLIFTON HOUSE, Va., April 9—9 P. M.

Hon. E. M. STANTON, Secretary of War:

The following correspondence has taken place between General Lee and myself.

There has been no relaxation in pursuit during its pendency.

U. S. GRANT, Lieut. Gen.

APRIL 9, 1865.

Gen. LEE, Commanding, etc.:

SIR: The result of the last week must convince you of the uselessness of further resistance on the part of the Army of Northern Virginia in this struggle, I feel like it is so and regard it as my duty to shift from myself the responsibility of any further effusion of blood, by asking of you the surrender of that portion of the Confederate States army known as the Army of Northern Virginia.

Very respectfully, your obedient servant,
U. S. GRANT,
Lieutenant General Commanding.

APRIL 7, 1865.

General: I have received your note of this date. Though not entirely of the opinion you express of the hopelessness of the further resistance on the part of the Army of Northern Virginia, I reciprocate your desire to avoid useless effusion of blood, and therefore before considering your proposition, ask the terms you will offer on condition of its surrender.

(Signed,) R. E. LEE, General.

To Lieut. Gen. Grant, commanding armies of the United States.

APRIL 8th, 1865.

General R. E. LEE, Commanding Confederate States army:

General: Your note of last evening, in reply to mine of same date, asking conditions on which I will accept the surrender of the Army of Northern Virginia is just received. In reply I will say that peace being my first desire, there is but one condition I insist upon, viz: that the men surrendered shall be disqualified for taking up arms again against the Government of the United States until properly exchanged. I will meet you or designate officers to meet any officers you may name for the purpose of arranging definitely the terms upon which the surrender of the Army of Northern Virginia will be received.

Very respectfully, etc.,
U. S. GRANT,
Lieut. Gen. commandidg U. S. Army.

APRIL 8th, 1865.

General: I received at a late hour your note of to-day in answer to mine of yesterday. I did not intend to propose the surrender of the Army of Northern Virginia, but to ask the terms of your proposition. To be frank, I do not think the emergency has arisen to call for the surrender of this Army, but as the restoration of peace should be the sole object of all, I desire to know whether your proposals would tend to that end. I would not, therefore, meet you with a view to surrender the Army of Northern Virginia, but as far as your proposition may affect the Confederate States forces under my command and tend to the restoration of peace. I should be pleased to meet you at 10 A. M., to-morrow, on old State road to Richmond, between the picket lines of the two armies. Very respectfully,

Your obedient servant,
R. E. LEE, General.

To Lieut. Gen. GRANT, Commanding, etc.

APRIL 9, 1865.

To Gen. R. E. LEE, Commanding, C. S. A:

Your note of yesterday is received. As I have no authority to treat on the subject of peace, the meeting proposed for 10 A. M., to-day could not lead to any good. I will state, however, General, that I am equally anxious for peace with yourself, and the whole North entertains the same feeling. The terms upon which peace can be had are well understood; by the South laying down their arms they will hasten that desirable event; save thousands of human lives and hundreds of millions of property not yet destroyed. Sincerely hoping that our difficulties may be settled without the loss of another life, I subscribe myself, very respectfully your obedient servant, U. S. GRANT,
Lieut. Gen., Commanding U. S. Army.

WAR DEPARTMENT, WASHINGTON, D. C.,
9:30 P. M., April 9, 1865.

To Lieutenant General Grant:

Thanks be to Almighty God for the great victory with which he has this day covered you and the gallant army under your command. The thanks of the Department, and of the Government, and of the people of the United States, their reverence and honor have been deserved, and will be given to you and the brave and gallant officers and soldiers of your commrnd, for all time. (Signed,)

E. M. STANTON, Secretary of War.

WAR DEPARTMENT, WASHINGTON, D. C.,
10 P. M., Apr l 9.

It is ordered that a salute of 200 guns be fired at the headquarters of every army and department, and at every post and arsenal in the United States, and at the Military Academy at West Point, on receipt of this order, in commemoration of the surrender of Gen. Lee and the Army of Northern Virginia to Lieut. Gen. Grant and the army under his command. Report, on the receipt of this order, to be made to the Adjutant General, Washington.

E. M. STANTON,
Secretary of War.

Glory to God in the Highest: Peace on Earth, Good will amongst men.

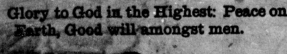

E PLURIBUS UNUM

EXTRA DISPATCH.

LEE'S SURRENDER!

FULL PARTICULARS.

Correspondence between Gens. Grant & Lee.

The Army of Northern Virginia Surrendered !!

The following correspondence concerning the most important event of the war, explains itself. It was dispatched to Gen. Pope from Washington this morning:

WASHINGTON, D. C., April 9, 1865.

To Maj. Gen DODGE:

This Department has just received the official report of the surrender this day of Gen. Lee and his army to Lieut General Grant, on the terms proposed by General Grant. Details will be given as speedily as possible Signed

E. M. STANTON,
Sec'y. of War.

HEADQ'RS ARMY OF UNITED STATES,
April 9, 1865 P. M.

To Hon. E. M. Stanton, Sec'y of War:

General Lee surrendered the Army of Northern Virginia this afternoon upon terms proposed by myself. The accompanying and additional correspondence will show the conditions fully.

(Signed) U. S. GRANT,
Lieut. General.

April 9, 1865.—*General:* I received your note of this morning on the picket line, whither I had come to meet you to ascertain definitely what terms were embraced in your propositions of yesterday with reference to the surrender of this army.

I now request an interview, in accordance with the offer contained in your letter of yesterday, for that purpose.

Very resp'y, Your ob't. s'vt.,
(Signed), R. E. LEE, Gen.

To Lt. Gen. U. S. Grant, Com'dg U. S A.

Your note of this date, is but this moment, 11:50 A. M. received. In consequence of my having passed from the Richmond and Lynchburg road, to the Fannville and Lynchburg I am thus writing about four miles of Walters Church and will push forward to the front for the purpose of meeting you. Notice sent to me on this road where you wish the interview to take place will meet me.

Very respectfully,
Your obedient servant,
U. S. GRANT, Lt. General.

APPOMATTOX COURT HOUSE, April 9, '65.

GENERAL R. E. LEE, Com'dg C. S. A.:

In accordance with the substance of my letter to you of the 8th inst, I propose to receive the surrender of the Army of Northern Virginia on the following terms, to-wit: Rolls of all the officers and men to be made in duplicate, one copy to be given to an officer designated by me, the other to be retained by such officer or officers as you may designate.

The officers to give their individual paroles not to take up arms against the Government of the United States, until properly exchanged, and each company or regimental commander sign a like parole for the men of their commands, the arms, artillery and public property to be parked or stacked, and turned over to the officers appointed by me to receive them. This will not embrace the side arms of the officers.

This done, such officer and men will be allowed to return to their homes, not to be disturbed by U. S. authority so long as they observe their paroles and the laws in force where they may reside.

Very respectfully,
U. S. GRANT, Lt. Gen.

H'DQRS. ARMY OF NORTHERN VA.,
April 9, 1865.

Lt. Gen. U. S. Grant, Com'dg, U. S. A.

General: I have received your letter of this date containing the terms of surrender of the Army of Northern Virginia, as proposed by you. As they are substantially the same as those expressed in your letter, of the 8th inst., they are accepted.

I will proceed to designate the proper officers to carry the stipulations into effect.

Very Resp'y, Your Ob't. S'vt,
R. E. LEE, Gen.

Further particulars in first Edition Evening Dispatch.

THIS WAS RICHMOND—Its ruins as seen across the James River in April, 1865. Courtesy Library of Congress.

NO URBAN RENEWAL—Devastated by war with no recourse or assistance through Federal aid. This was Richmond in the spring of 1865. Courtesy Library of Congress.

GENERAL ROBERT E. LEE AT HOME IN RICHMOND, APRIL, 1865—With his son Major General George Washington Custis Lee on his right and Colonel Walter Taylor on his left he poses shortly after the surrender at Appomattox. As General-in-Chief of the Confederate forces Lee was universally beloved by Southern soldiers and civilians. Brady photo, courtesy Library of Congress.

137

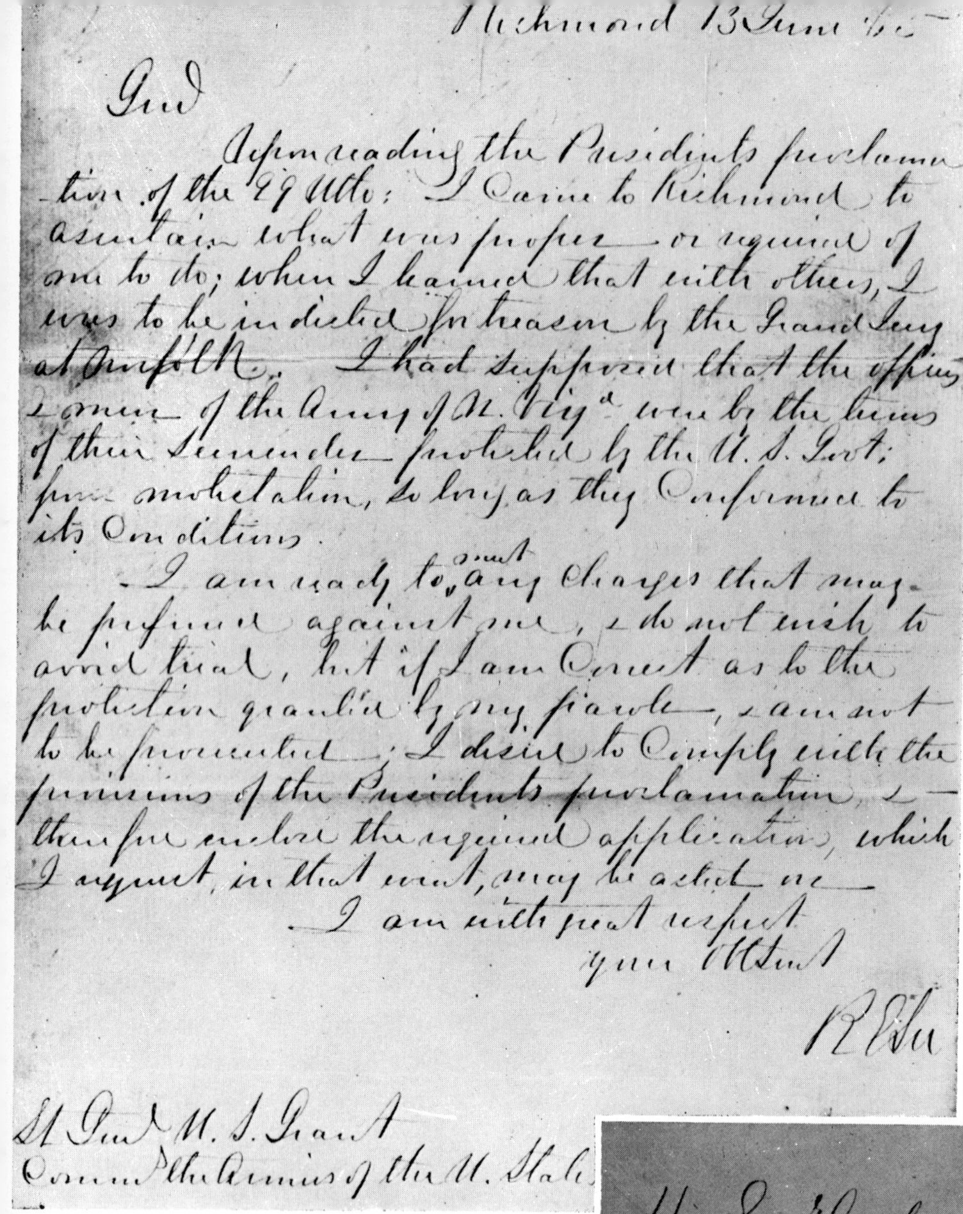

Richmond 13 June '65

Genl

Upon reading the Presidents proclamation of the 29 Ulto: I came to Richmond to ascertain what was proper or required of me to do; when I learned that with others, I was to be indicted for treason by the Grand Jury at Norfolk. I had supposed that the officers & men of the Army of N. Virga were by the terms of their surrender protected by the U.S. Govt: from molestation, so long as they conformed to its conditions.

I am ready to meet any charges that may be preferred against me, & do not wish to avoid trial, but if I am correct as to the protection granted by my parole, & am not to be prosecuted; I desire to comply with the provisions of the Presidents proclamation, & therefore enclose the required application, which I request, in that event, may be acted on

I am with great respect
your obt Servt

R E Lee

Lt Genl U. S. Grant
Comdg the Armies of the U. States

LEE REQUESTS THE AMNESTY GUARANTEED BY GRANT — General Grant gave his full support to Lee's request for full protection under the terms of his parole. Courtesy Illinois State Historical Library.

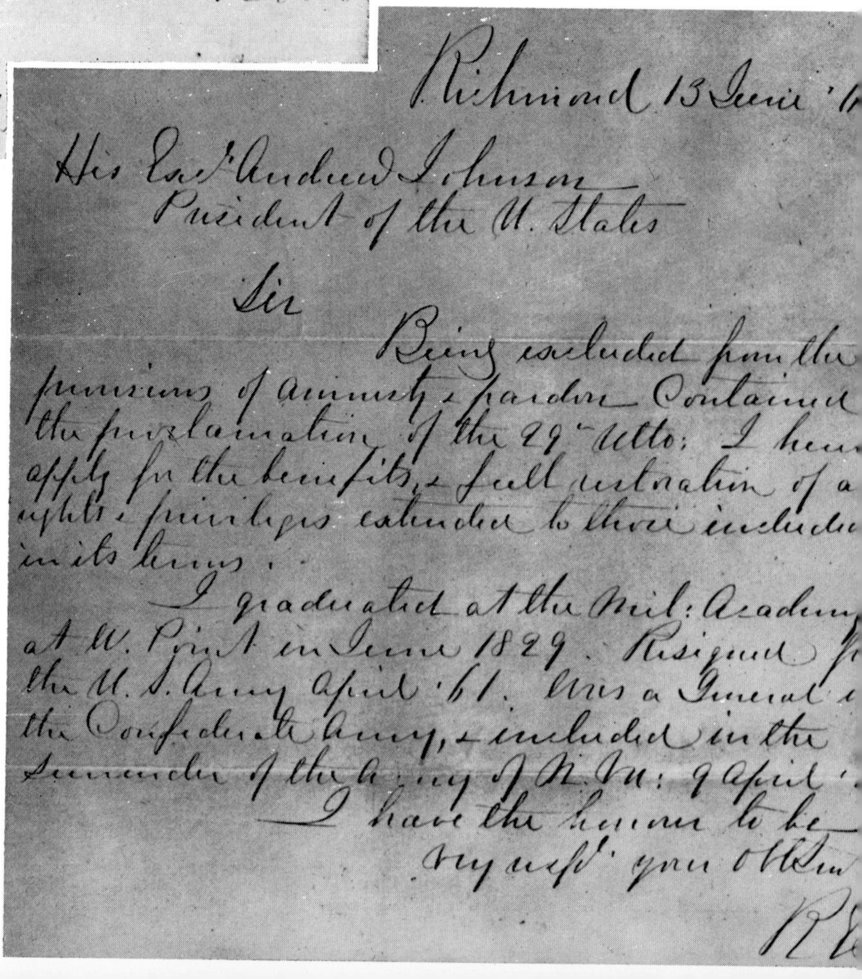

Richmond 13 June '6

His Excy Andrew Johnson
President of the U. States

Sir

Being excluded from the provisions of Amnesty & pardon contained the proclamation of the 29 Ulto: I hereby apply for the benefits, & full restoration of all rights & privileges extended to those included in its terms.

I graduated at the Mil: Academy at W. Point in June 1829. Resigned from the U. S. Army April '61. Was a General in the Confederate Army, & included in the surrender of the Army of N. Va: 9 April

I have the honor to be very respy your obt Servt

R E Lee

S. 29. Acfs 1865.
Richmond, 13th June '65

Lee, R. E.

(Understanding that, with others, he is to be indicted for treason by the Grand Jury at Norfolk, states his readiness to meet any charges that may be brought forward. Had supposed that the terms of his surrender protected him. If they should, he desires to comply with provisions of amnesty proclamation and therefore encloses the required application which in that event he requests may be acted on.

one enclosure

Recd Acfs. June 16 1865.

Respectfully forwarded to the Sec't of War.

In my opinion the officers and men paroled at Appomattox C.H. and since upon the same terms given to Lee, cannot be tried for treason so long as they observed the terms of their parole. This is my understanding. Good faith as well as true policy dictates that we should observe the conditions of that convention. Bad faith on the part of the Government or a construction of that convention subjecting officers to trial for treason, would produce a feeling of insecurity in the minds of all paroled officers and men. If so disposed they might even regard such an infraction of terms by the Government as an entire release from all obligation on their part.

I will state further that the terms granted by me met with the hearty approval of the President at the time and of the country generally. The action of Judge Underwood in Norfolk has already had an injurious effect, and I would ask that he be ordered to quash all indictments found against paroled prisoners of war, and to desist from further prosecution of them

U. S. Grant

Hdqn. Acfs. June 16. 65. Lieut. General

GRAND REVIEW IN WASHINGTON, D.C.—1865. Pennsylvania Avenue was a beehive on May 24th and 25th. Courtesy Library of Congress.

Chapter Eleven

Penchant For Peace

President Andrew Johnson was a southern Jacksonian Democrat in thought and principle from Tennessee, who had become a Republican in name only. An intense Unionist, his first actions as President made him appear to be siding with the Radical Republicans. He first opined that all rebel leaders should be hanged. Later he reversed himself by a May 29th proclamation of general amnesty that pardoned all of the Confederacy below the rank of general or those with a fortune of less than $20,000. Those exceptions to the general pardon were required to obtain Presidential pardons—an act that was repeated with great generosity.

His leniency caused the Radicals to oppose him vehemently. They were well led and ruthless in their opposition. Johnson's temper and biting tongue lost him the support of his party's leaders. Soon (in the spring of 1868) he would be tried by the Senate for impeachment. The conviction failed by one vote of the two-thirds majority required. He had dismissed Secretary of War Stanton who had refused to resign. It was alleged Johnson had violated the Tenure of Office Act passed by the Radicals to restrict him. It is interesting to note that this act in effect was declared unconstitutional by the Supreme Court in 1926.

Grant had misgivings about conditions in Mexico. In defiance of the Monroe Doctrine, the Archduke Maximilian, backed by his French troops, had placed himself on the throne of Mexico. Weakened by her various revolutions, Mexico had been unable to protect visiting citizens from foreign countries. Pretending to protect her citizens, France had seized Mexico while we were in the throes of a civil war. The invaded country's rights had been totally disregarded by France, England and Spain.

Repeatedly, Grant had spoken of the condition to both Lincoln and Stanton. Neither had expressed a view, for they had problems of their own. With these problems largely under control, Grant saw no reason to permit this threat to our southern border to continue. Immediately following the surrender of Lee, on the first day of the Grand Review in Washington, he ordered Sheridan with a corps to Texas, giving him secret orders to watch the course of events on the Rio Grande. It was Grant's hope to help Juarez expel the French troops from Mexico, a hope that was defeated by Secretary of State William H. Seward. Seward wished to, and did, solve the matter by diplomatic means.

Mrs. Sherman had asked Grant to contribute to a benefit fair in Chicago for disabled soldiers and their families. His cream-colored horse, "Old Jack," which he had ridden at

Fort Donelson, was given to be raffled. Attending the fair in June, he rode Jack around the fairgrounds to the cheers of the huge crowd present. When Governor Yates asked him to speak, he refused. Speaking and dancing never had been his accomplishments.

Returning to Boston July 31st, he received a tremendous demonstration at Faneuil Hall. The City of Boston presented him with a $5,000 library.

He was wildly received on his tour through New England. Returning to Galena, a bipartisan crowd estimated at 25,000 observed the Republican citizens committee present him and his family with a well-furnished brick residence that had been constructed after raising $16,000 by subscription. The Democratic Mayor and Councilmen, having been ignored in the reception plans, courteously "forgot" to give Grant a key to the city.

WHEN GRANT WENT HOME—On August 18, 1865, Galena showed Grant it cared. This arch extended across Main Street. The large five-story building on the right is the DeSoto House. Photographed by E. W. Peirce, courtesy Illinois State Historical Library.

"HAIL TO THE CHIEF WHO IN TRIUMPH ADVANCES."

HE GOT HIS SIDEWALK—On one occasion Grant had said that his greatest political ambition was to be the mayor of Galena so that he might try to induce the council to build a sidewalk up to his house. When he arrived in Galena in August of 1865 he was greeted by this arch. Courtesy Illinois State Historical Library.

GALENA'S FINEST—This hotel, then at the peak of its career, banqueted some 500 people honoring General Grant. General John A. Logan gave the principal address from the DeSoto House balcony where Abraham Lincoln once had given a campaign speech. From a DeSoto House bill of fare, 1855. Courtesy Galena Historical Society.

After several weeks in their new home, Grant headed to Washington via Cincinnati, Covington, Bethel and Georgetown, arriving at his Eye Street residence in Washington that October.

He had been offered a home by the citizens of Philadelphia with the understanding he would live there. After he offered to return it, they asked him to accept it, recognizing he had to live near his Washington headquarters. New York City gave him $100,000.

The economy-minded Grant closed unneeded hospitals, dispensaries and other buildings, sold surplus stores and equipment and reduced the numbers of employes as much as could be done practically. In a short time he had reduced his department's monthly expenses $407,000, making an annual savings of almost $5,000,000. Under his close scrutiny the manufacture of heavy arms was curtailed. Rigid economy was the order of the day.

On July 25, 1866, Congress made Grant the first full (four-star) general since George Washington. The army was to have one lieutenant general, five major generals, ten regiments of cavalry, five of artillery and 45 of infantry, in all, 54,641 men.

Early that year Johnson had appointed Grant's oldest son, Fred, a cadet-at-large to West Point. In spite of this gesture Grant's views were so far removed from Johnson's that the latter decided to send him on a mission to Mexico. Grant politely refused to go. At a Cabinet meeting detailed instructions were read to him by the Secretary of State just as though he had not refused. Before all of the Cabinet members Grant indicated his unwillingness to go. The angered President requested a ruling from the Attorney General. Grant said he could answer that question—that since he

was a military officer he was bound to obey any miiltary order. Since this was a civil or diplomatic mission he was not required to take the assignment, and did not intend to. And he didn't.

The American people were learning of their great loss in the death of Lincoln, for the contrast between him and his successor was becoming more evident. Johnson's wrangling, his frequent loss of temper and dignity, did not endear him.

Desiring another term, Johnson prepared for a political junket. Leaving Washington on August 28, 1866, with Secretary of Navy Gideon Welles, Postmaster General Randall, General Grant, Admiral David Farragut, General Custer, Secretary William Seward and their wives amongst others, Johnson went on a tour of New England, where he was well received. His political progress enraged the Radicals, for his speaking theme had been "the sanctity of the Constitution and the Union." He continued his trip to Chicago, on what he called "swinging around the circle," there to lay a cornerstone on September 6th for the Stephen A. Douglas monument.

At St. Louis, Indianapolis, throughout Ohio into Cleveland and at Pittsburgh, a rough element hurled insults and heckled to a point that he responded with a barbed tongue and undignified repartee. James G. Blaine observed: "With whatever strength or prestige the President left Washington, he certainly returned to the Capitol personally discredited and politically ruined." Grant, Farragut and Custer had been ordered to go along as window dressing, Johnson displaying these popular idols at every opportunity.

Stanton, though a fanatical patriot and Bible student, was an intolerant, domineering, power-

MAJOR GENERAL JOHN A. LOGAN—Capable politician, gallant and efficient officer, outstanding orator, and a friend of Grant. Photo by John Goldin, Washington, D.C., 1865. Ccurtesy Col. Brice C. W. Custer.

FIRST FOUR-STAR GENERAL—Congress approved the new rank in 1866 to which Grant was immediately appointed. Courtesy The Smithsonian Institution.

hungry opponent of Johnson. With the dominant Radicals behind him, he bucked and battered the President's project to restore the South to full power. Johnson could think of one weapon to use against the Stanton tactics—get rid of him. He had inherited him from Lincoln.

On Monday morning, August 5, 1867, President Johnson demanded that Stanton resign as Secretary of War. Stanton refused, as was his right under the Tenure of Office Act that had been passed over the President's veto on March 2nd. One week later, on August 12, Johnson appointed Grant Secretary of War *ad interim*, which office he held reluctantly for five months while performing, at the same time, the duties of General-in-Chief. The Senate passed a resolution January 13, 1868, *not* sustaining the President's action. The breach between Grant and Johnson then became permanent, placing Grant in the position of political opposition—and making him a potential candidate of the Republican party for President.

A GIFT FROM GALENA—At the close of the ceremonies at the Grant homecoming Ulysses was given the key to this house on the east side of the Galena River. The house was a gift of the townsfolk, some $16,000 being raised by subscription to construct and furnish it. It is carefully maintained by the State of Illinois, fully furnished, and open to visitors each day. Courtesy Chicago Historical Society.

AT HOME WITH HIS SON AND HIS CIGAR—Ulysses enjoying the sunlight with his small son Jesse on the porch of his Galena home. In all likelihood, Julia had requested that he smoke his cigar on the outside of their new home. Photo from a Carbutt stereo. Courtesy Chicago Historical Society.

GRANT RESIDENCE IN WASHINGTON, D. C.—Following the war Grant's duties as General-in-Chief required his almost continual presence at the Capitol. This home was on I Street between Second and Third Street Northwest.

General Grant once expressed a desire to live in Philadelphia. A leading merchant, George H. Stuart, began a movement to gather funds amongst Philadelphia residents to obtain a home for Grant. Raising $50,000, a residence was selected and lavishly furnished at 2009 Chestnut Street. On April 12, 1865, at a surprise gathering, the home was presented to Grant with an engrossed deed in a jeweled case. Shortly afterward he moved to Washington where his duties kept him most of the time. Brady photo, courtesy National Archives.

NELLIE GRANT—Christened Ellen Wrenshall Grant, she was born on the Dent farm July 4, 1855. Photo by E. W. Pierce, Galena, 1865. Courtesy State Historical Society of Colorado Library.

MILITARY COAT WORN BY GENERAL GRANT—Courtesy West Point Museum Collections.

BOOTS WORN BY GRANT 1864-1865—Courtesy the Smithsonian Institution.

FIELD GLASSES USED BY GRANT—

(A) Glasses with case, courtesy the Smithsonian Institution.

(B) Extra long field glasses, courtesy West Point Museum Collections.

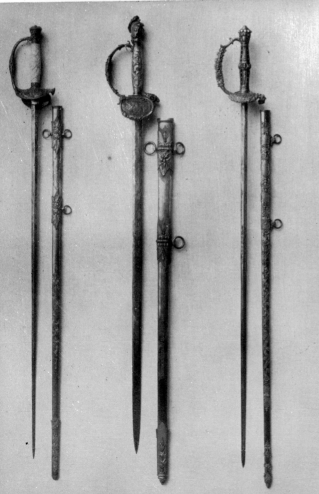

SHOULDER STRAPS WORN BY U. S. GRANT—

(A) Two-star rank of major general of volunteers, February 17, 1862. Courtesy West Point Museum Collections.

(B) Three-star rank of lieutenant general, March 2, 1864. Shoulder straps were worn during campaigns of Richmond and Petersburg. Courtesy The Smithsonian Institution.

(C) Four-star rank of general, July 25, 1866. Courtesy Military Order of Loyal Legion.

GENERAL GRANT'S ARMY LANTERN—Courtesy West Point Museum Collections.

PRESENTATION SWORDS—Top: Sword presented to Gen. Grant in 1836 by citizens of Jo Daviess County, Ill.; Middle: Sword presented to Grant in 1864 by the U. S. Sanitary Commission; Bottom: Sword presented to Grant in 1861 in Galena by G. W. Graham, C. B. Lagow, C. C. March and John Cook. Courtesy The Smithsonian Institution.

The **GRANT FAMILY IN 1867**—Painted by W. Cogswell, 1867. Courtesy The Smithsonian Institution.

GRANT FAMILY IN 1866—From a watercolor by John Slater. Courtesy Detroit Historical Museum.

GENERAL GRANT AT FORT SANDERS, WYOMING—General Grenville Dodge had invited Grant and the others shown in this 1867 photograph to discuss the building of the Union Pacific Railroad, which had not reached Laramie. Courtesy State Historical Society of Colorado Library.

Chapter Twelve

Potomac Fever

Both parties were looking for a presidential candidate. The Republicans were disenchanted with their man Johnson; the Democrats hoped to depose him with a vote-attracting opponent.

Early in the spring of 1867, Senator Benjamin F. Wade had visited Covington, Kentucky, to inquire as to Grant's political leanings. What better person to talk to than Grant's brother-in-law, the Reverend Michael J. Cramer? At the time Cramer, who had married Ulysses' sister Mary, was residing with Jesse Grant. Cramer advised Wade that Grant endorsed all Congressional measures and was a thorough Republican. At the conclusion of their conversation Wade said: "That settles the matter; we shall propose Grant as the candidate of the Republican party for the Presidency."

Though Grant gave no outward indication that he was the least bit inclined toward a political career until his break with Johnson, the press and the politicians, who were out of patience with the administration, began to press for his nomination.

Secretary of Navy Gideon Welles had a long talk with Grant late that August. Welles was alarmed "to see how little he understood of the fundamental principles and structure of our government, and of the Constitution itself." It appeared that Grant believed Congress to be a central power above the Constitution. He did not favor giving voting privileges to the rebels for fear they would "take the government of their states into their own hands." He looked upon Southern states as territories that should be "admitted into the Union when we felt we could trust them."

In his *Diary* Welles wrote: "General Grant has become severely afflicted with Presidential disease, and it warps his judgment, which is not very intelligent or enlightened at best. He is less sound on great and fundamental principles, vastly less informed, than I had supposed possible for a man of his opportunities."

The Republican National Convention in 1868 was held in Chicago. On May 21st, General Lucius Fairchild of Wisconsin headed a delegation of soldiers and sailors presenting a resolution endorsing General U. S. Grant. Amid great applause, Henry S. Lane of Indiana leaped upon a chair and moved that Grant be nominated by acclamation. The response was immediate. Without rules, he was acclaimed their nominee. Schuyler Colfax, Speaker of the House of Representatives, was selected as his Vice Presidential running mate.

Grant held Colfax in high esteem. He considered him "the most popular man in the country, and the only thing the Democrats can accuse him of is that he is a Republican."

The Republican platform was a nebulous thing that said little more than denounce all attempts to repudiate the public debt. Grant did more for the campaign in his letter of acceptance May 29th than the platform did, by ending his letter with "Let us have peace." This phrase became the Republican slogan.

On July 9, 1868, the Democrats nominated for President former Governor of New York Horatio Seymour; and for Vice President, one of Grant's former commanders, Francis P. Blair Jr. of Missouri.

A week later Grant, in company with Sherman and Sheridan, started over the Kansas Pacific Railroad along the Smoky Hill route to Denver. Grant wanted to see at first hand the problems involved in dealing with the Indian depredations in that area. Commissioner General Buford had traced the cause of the Indian outbreak of 1867 to Major General Hancock's expedition to Fort Larned, and to his burning of the Indian camp on Pawnee Fork in April of that year. A Peace Commission, of which Sherman was the dissenting member, had suggested that Hancock had created the dilemma. Grant observed to Sherman that the citizens around the various forts, in making their complaints of

Indian depredations, acted entirely from selfish motives, and that it would be advisable to rely upon inspections of competent officers to aid in dealing with Indians and in the disposition of troops. As a Presidential candidate Grant left the train at Cheyenne Wells, taking a stage coach to Denver.

Grant and his family, at Congressman Washburne's suggestion, repaired to Galena a second time. Arriving there August 7th, they remained at home throughout the election campaign.

The election of November 3rd gave the war hero a majority of only 306,000 of a total vote of 5,715,000 votes, winning him the electoral votes of 26 of the 34 states. His electoral college vote was 214 as compared to Seymour's 80.

Grant fostered some unorthodox ideas about making appointments to his Cabinet. He selected men as he selected his generals or his staff—not necessarily on fitness, training or ability—rather on their acceptability to him. He consulted no one, and wanted no advice in making these appointments. This deeply offended party leaders, and reflected upon them and their party when important posts were filled by the unqualified. To add to the confusion, Grant believed it indelicate to consult with individuals he proposed appointing

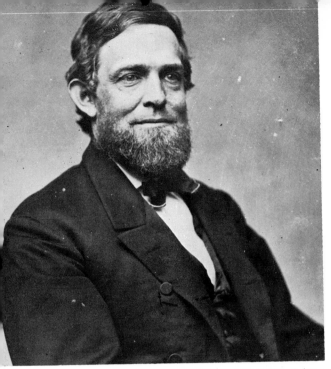

GIDEON WELLES, LINCOLN'S SECRETARY OF THE NAVY—A bitter critic of Grant for his explanation to the President and Cabinet of his resignation from the office of Secretary of War, he wrote in his **Diary** that it "is throughout highly discreditable to Grant's integrity, honor, ability and truth. . . ." Courtesy Library of Congress.

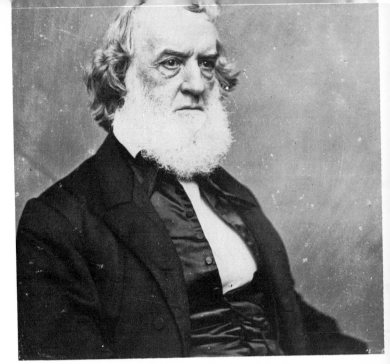

VICE PRESIDENT SCHUYLER COLFAX—As Speaker of the House of Representatives he was Grant's running mate in the election of 1868. Courtesy Library of Congress.

until he announced sending their names to the Senate for confirmation. Consequently, his Cabinet appointments were a source of astonishment. He wanted to govern without politics.

He surrounded himself with a bevy of secretaries, who were, predominantly, military aids, and who shielded him from the many influencial men who sought to reach him, much to their exasperation. And though charged with nepotism, he appointed only eight members of his family to governmental positions during his eight years in office. None were of importance. Yet Senator Charles Sumner, a bitter opponent of anything Grant stood for had exploited the alleged nepotism and had charged additionally that there had been improper acceptance of gifts.

True, Grant had accepted cigars and other small items, and a home from several grateful communities. The latter had been accepted prior to any mention of a political career, and with no strings expressed or implied. At no time in his life could Grant ever be accused of being dishonest. But once in the political stream the recipient must always question the propriety of accepting a gift. Gratitude can color judgment. The size of a gift generally is unimportant.

Unfortunately Grant became President at exactly the wrong time. He had neither background nor aptitude for governing or politics. A country beset

with problems that would have been monumental to Lincoln, Jefferson or Hamilton, was saddled with a military hero whose only claim to office was his ability to capture the popular vote.

The country was in a moral ebbtide. Money talked and, seemingly, everyone was out for the "fast buck." The quest for the dollar had entered the sphere of politics. Grant, who was honesty itself, was naive and trusting enough to suspect no one, at least in the beginning.

Following his persistent and indiscreet lobbying, personal visits and pressure on Senators to obtain their approval on the annexation of the island of San Domingo, which failed through lack of support, the Credit Mobilier scandal broke. The "Teapot Dome" of 1872, it wrecked the reputations of many in high places including Vice President Schuyler Colfax. Colfax was confronted with a $1,200 cancelled check made out to him on stock he claimed he had never received. Grant wrote him, in the face of evidence to the contrary, that he was convinced he was innocent.

Grant always had a warm spot in his heart for the Indians. Their unjust treatment by the whites he had observed when he had been stationed on the West Coast in 1852. Feeling strongly enough to do something about it he announced his new Indian Policy in his second annual message to Congress in 1870. Thereafter religious groups would nominate all agents. The agents would civilize and Christianize the Indians. All Indians would be maintained on their reservations, where they would live in houses and go to schools and churches.

On June 6th the President and Mrs. Grant held a gala reception in the East Room of the White House for a Sioux Indian delegation consisting of Ogallala Chief Red Cloud with 17 of his chiefs, three of his wives and Brulé Chief Spotted Tail with four of his chiefs.

After the dinner had been served, Spotted Tail mentioned that the food white men were eating was better than they doled out to the Indians. The interpreter indicated that the white man was so rewarded because he had abandoned the warpath for farming. Spotted Tail responded: "Haw! I will quit the warpath if you will always treat me like this and let me live in as big a house." This was too much for Grant, who burst into a hearty laugh.

Two days later, at a meeting in the Executive Office, the chiefs demanded the abandonment of Fort Fetterman. Previously they had been advised the government wanted only peace, to which Red Cloud had replied that it would be forthcoming if Fort Fetterman was removed. Grant emphasized that it must remain for the protection of both Indians and white men.

Grant showed early indications of financial conservatism. On March 18, 1869, he signed his first law, an act pledging the government's gold to redeem greenbacks issued during the Civil War. And on September 24, 1869, he ordered the sale of four million dollars of Treasury gold to upset the scheme of two speculators, Jay Gould and James Fish Jr., who attempted to corner the gold supply, run the price up to 200, then sell. Grant's friendly association with Gould made it appear he was involved in the scheme, but he was not. Though Grant defeated their plan, his previous association with them made many doubt him.

DETROIT MAKES ITS WANTS KNOWN—Poster courtesy Detroit Historical Museum.

A NATION MAKES ITS WANTS KNOWN—Courtesy Detroit Historical Museum.

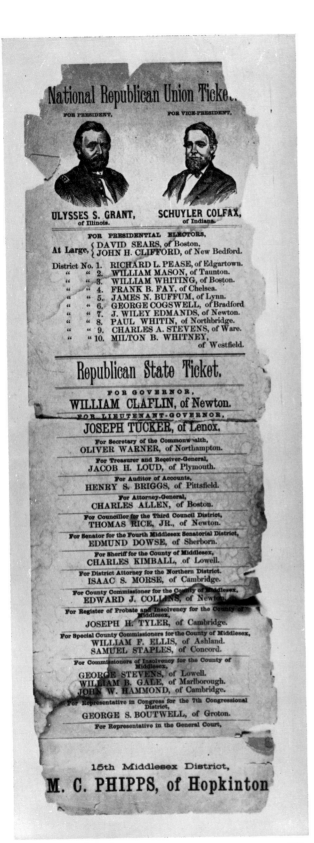

National Republican Union Ticket.

FOR PRESIDENT,   **FOR VICE-PRESIDENT,**

ULYSSES S. GRANT, of Illinois.   **SCHUYLER COLFAX,** of Indiana.

FOR PRESIDENTIAL ELECTORS,

At Large, { DAVID SEARS, of Boston, JOHN H. CLIFFORD, of New Bedford.

District No. 1.   RICHARD L. PEASE, of Edgartown.
   "   " 2.   WILLIAM MASON, of Taunton.
   "   " 3.   WILLIAM WHITING, of Boston.
   "   " 4.   FRANK B. FAY, of Chelsea.
   "   " 5.   JAMES N. BUFFUM, of Lynn.
   "   " 6.   GEORGE COGSWELL, of Bradford.
   "   " 7.   J. WILEY EDMANDS, of Newton.
   "   " 8.   PAUL WHITIN, of Northbridge.
   "   " 9.   CHARLES A. STEVENS, of Ware.
   "   " 10.   MILTON B. WHITNEY, of Westfield.

Republican State Ticket.

FOR GOVERNOR,
WILLIAM CLAFLIN, of Newton.

FOR LIEUTENANT-GOVERNOR,
JOSEPH TUCKER, of Lenox.

For Secretary of the Commonwealth,
OLIVER WARNER, of Northampton.

For Treasurer and Receiver-General,
JACOB H. LOUD, of Plymouth.

For Auditor of Accounts,
HENRY S. BRIGGS, of Pittsfield.

For Attorney-General,
CHARLES ALLEN, of Boston.

For Councillor for the Third Council District,
THOMAS RICE, JR., of Newton.

For Senator for the Fourth Middlesex Senatorial District,
EDMUND DOWSE, of Sherborn.

For Sheriff for the County of Middlesex,
CHARLES KIMBALL, of Lowell.

For District Attorney for the Northern District,
ISAAC S. MORSE, of Cambridge.

For County Commissioner for the County of Middlesex,
EDWARD J. COLLINS, of Newton.

For Register of Probate and Insolvency for the County of Middlesex,
JOSEPH H. TYLER, of Cambridge.

For Special County Commissioners for the County of Middlesex,
WILLIAM F. ELLIS, of Ashland.
SAMUEL STAPLES, of Concord.

For Commissioners of Insolvency for the County of Middlesex,
GEORGE STEVENS, of Lowell.
WILLIAM B. GALE, of Marlborough.
JOHN W. HAMMOND, of Cambridge.

For Representative in Congress for the 7th Congressional District,
GEORGE S. BOUTWELL, of Groton.

For Representative in the General Court,

15th Middlesex District,
M. C. PHIPPS, of Hopkinton

IN THE 1868 ELECTION IT'S GRANT BOTH EAST AND WEST—
MASSACHUSETTS REPUBLICAN TICKET.
REPUBLICAN TICKET. Courtesy The Smithsonian Institution.
MISSOURI TICKET—Courtesy Missouri Historical Society.

Republican Ticket.

For President, . . . ULYSSES S. GRANT.
For Vice-President, . . SCHUYLER COLFAX.

OUR COUNTRY'S DEFENDERS.

I propose to move immediately upon your works.—Grant.

For Electors of President and Vice-President,

AMOS PAUL,   South-Newmarket.
JOEL EASTMAN,   Conway.
MASON W. TAPPAN,   Bradford.
EDWARD L. GODDARD,   Claremont.
ALBERT M. SHAW,   Lebanon.

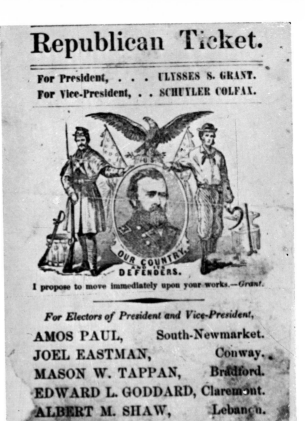

2d Representative District.

LET US HAVE PEACE!
TO THE POLLS   FOR GRANT & COLFAX
COPYRIGHT SECURED BY THE RADICAL STATE COMM.

FOR PRESIDENT,
ULYSSES S. GRANT.
FOR VICE-PRESIDENT,
SCHUYLER COLFAX.

For Presidential Electors at Large,
CARL SCHURZ,
J. D. HINES.

For Presidential District Electors,

CHAUNCEY I. FILLEY,   THOS. E. BASSETT,
GEORGE HUSMANN,   LOUIS GEORGENS,
E. S. WATERBURY,   LEWIS H. WEATHERBY,
J. P. TRACY,   A. J. BAKER,
     THEODORE BRUERE.

For Congress,
GUSTAVUS A. FINKELNBURG.

STATE OFFICERS.

For Governor................JOSEPH W. McCLURG
For Lieutenant Governor.....EDWIN O. STANARD
For Secretary of State......FRANCIS RODMAN
For Treasurer...............W. Q. DALLMEYER
For Auditor.................DANIEL M. DRAPER
For Register of Lands.......JOSEPH H. McGEE
For Attorney General........HORACE B. JOHNSON
For Supreme Judges { DAVID WAGNER
              PHILEMON BLISS
              WARREN CURRIER

Constitutional Amendment—Yes.

COUNTY OFFICERS.

For State Senator...............LOUIS GOTTSCHALK
For Representative..............FREDERICK ROEYER
For Supervisor of Registration..HENRY RATHJEN
For Judges of St. Louis { RODERICK E. ROMBAUER
   Circuit Court.   IRWIN Z. SMITH
                JAMES K. KNIGHT
For Judge of the Probate Court...JOSEPH P. YASTINE
For Public Administrator.........HENRY GAMBS
For Sheriff......................JOHN McNEIL
For Coroner......................JOSEPH SPIEGELHALTER
For County Marshal...............JOHN McFALL
For County Surveyor..............JULIUS PITZMAN
For Circuit Attorney.............CHARLES P. JOHNSON
For Assistant Circuit Attorney...WILLIAM KREUTER
For County Superintendent } ANDREW W. MURPHY
   of Public Schools.

TOWNSHIP OFFICERS.

For Justice of the Peace.........CHARLES PICKER
For Constable....................THEODORE HORMANN

For the Railroad Subscription.

GRANT CAMPAIGN BUTTONS, TOKENS AND MEDALS—
(A) Schuyler Colfax Daguerreotype, 1886-1869, black, blue and white. Courtesy American Numismatic Society.
(B) U. S. Grant silver medal, 1868. Courtesy American Numismatic Society.
(C) U. S. Grant and S. Colfax medal, 1873 by Emil Segel. Courtesy American Numismatic Society.
(D) Courtesy The Smithsonian Institution.
(E) Courtesy The Smithsonian Institution .
(F) Medal 1897 issued by American Numismatic and Archaeological Society. Courtesy American Numismatic Society.
(G) Medal given by the City of Geneva, Switzerland during Grant's world tour. Courtesy American Numismatic Society.
(H) Lead medal commemorating Grant reception in Philadelphia, 1879. Courtesy American Numismatic Society.
(I) Small silver medal without date is of Lieut. Gen. U. S. Grant, Commander U. S. Army.
Large aluminum medal commemorates the unveiling of the Grant monument in Lincoln Park, Chicago, Ill., 1891.
Courtesy American Numismatic Society.
(J) Bronze medal, 1892, of Father Washington, Saviour Lincoln, and Defender Grant. Courtesy American Numismatic Society.

SECRETARY OF THE TREASURY FOR A DAY—Alexander Turney Stewart, wealthy New York dry goods merchant, though appointed by Grant, could not hold the office because of an old statute that prohibited a merchant from heading a financial system. Courtesy New York Historical Society, New York City.

DEMOCRATIC PRESIDENTIAL ASPIRANT—Horatio Seymour, former governor of New York, opposed Grant in 1868. J. Gurney & Sons photo, 1868. Courtesy The New York Historical Society, New York City.

POSTMASTER GENERAL—John A. J. Creswell was sworn in March 5, 1869. Courtesy Library of Congress. **SECRETARY OF THE NAVY** Adolph Edward Borie of Pennsylvania took over on March 9, 1869. Courtesy Library of Congress. **GEORGE SEWALL BOUTWELL**—This Massachusetts Senator had been the first Commissioner of Internal Revenue in 1862-1863. He was made Secretary of the Treasury March 11, 1869. Courtesy Library of Congress. **SECRETARY OF STATE**—Hamilton Fish of New York served in this capacity from March 11, 1869 until 1877. The scholarly gentleman served Grant with great capacity. Courtesy Library of Congress. **BENJAMIN H. BRISTOW**—This Kentucky lawyer was appointed Secretary of the Treasury in June, 1874. Shrewd and concientious, he soon uncovered evidence against the Whiskey Ring which involved Grant's principal secretary, General Orville E. Babcock. Courtesy Library of Congress. **SECRETARY OF THE INTERIOR**—Jacob Dolson Cox of Ohio entered the office March 9, 1869. Courtesy Library of Congress. **WILLIAM WORTH BELKNAP**—From Iowa, he was made Secretary of War October 25, 1869. Courtesy Library of Congress. **MAJOR GENERAL JOHN A. RAWLINS**—Rawlins, who had served on Grant's staff from the very beginning, was dying from tuberculosis when appointed Secretary of War March 11, 1869. He was succeeded by General Sherman that September who was followed on October 25th by Belknap. Brady photo, courtesy Library of Congress. **BRIGADIER GENERAL FREDERICK T. DENT**—Serving in no great capacity on the military staff it seemed natural that this chum and brother-in-law of Grant's would be a member of his White House staff. Courtesy Library of Congress. **BRIGADIER GENERAL ADAM BADEAU**—As Grant's military secretary preparing his military memoirs he continued in this capacity in the White House. Though having no part of politics and politicians he was sent to San Domingo to sound out its officials on the question of annexation by the United States. Courtesy Library of Congress. **BRIGADIER GENERAL ORVILLE E. BABCOCK**—As Grant's principal secretary he was in a position of great trust and temptation. Yielding to the overtures of the Whiskey Ring, as uncovered by the investigation of Secretary of the Treasury Bristow, he was brought to trial. Grant made a mockery of it by testifying that he believed Babcock to be guiltless in thought or deed. Courtesy Library of Congress.

155

PRESIDENT GRANT'S CABINET IN SESSION—Left to right: Jacob D. Cox, Hamilton Fish, John A. Rawlins, President Grant, George S. Boutwell, Adolph E. Borie, and Ebenezer R. Hoar (Attorney General). Drawn by W. S. L. Jewett for Harper's Weekly, 1869. Courtesy Library of Congress.

GRANT INAUGURATION IN 1869—March 4th was the beginning of a new career. Grant accepted the office without fear, with no knowledge of the problems he would face. Courtesy Library of Congress.

INAUGURAL BALL IN 1869—Arrival of President Grant and his wife at the Treasury Department. Sketch by James E. Taylor for Frank Leslie's Illustrated weekly, 1869. Courtesy Library of Congress.

DEMOCRATIC AND LIBERAL REPUBLICAN NOMINEE FOR PRESIDENT—Horace Greeley, editor of the New York Tribune, was backed by a large group of intellectuals and reformers of both parties who opposed both the moneyed interests and an anti-Southern group that seemed to control Grant. Courtesy The New York Historical Society, New York City.

VICE PRESIDENT HENRY WILSON—Grant's running-mate in the 1868 election. He was from Massachusetts. Brady photo, courtesy Ansco Historical Collections.

WHY THEY DON'T LIKE HIM—Harper's Weekly, September 16, 1871. Courtesy Ohio Historical Society.

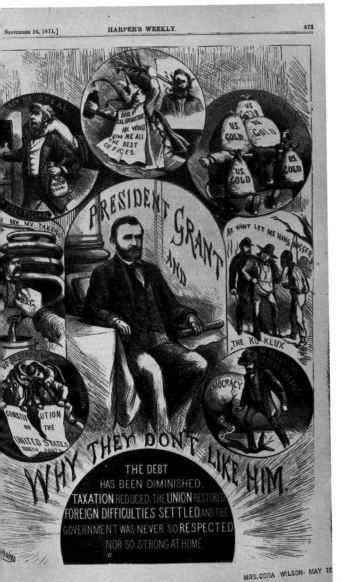

THE WORKINGMAN'S BANNER—Currier & Ives Lithograph, 1872, courtesy Library of Congress.

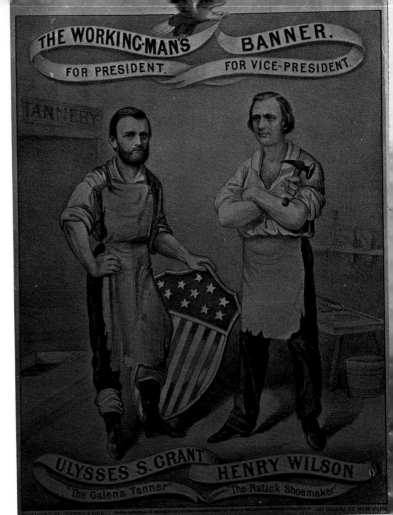

A POPULAR VERDICT—A Democratic cartoon. Courtesy Ohio Historical Society.

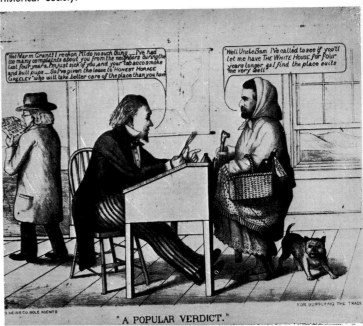

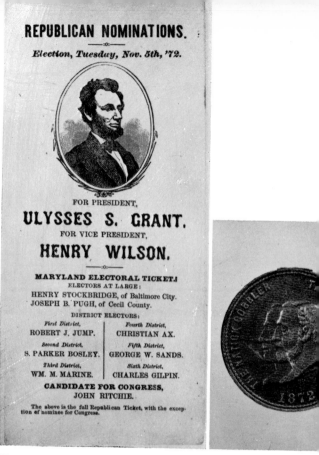

GRANT AND WILSON—(A) Maryland Electoral Ticket, courtesy The Smithsonian Institution. (B) Leather medal—"Grant and Wilson; The Natick Cobler & The Galena Tanner." Courtesy The American Numismatic Society.

JOHN ALEXANDER LOGAN AND FAMILY—A Congressman and Senator, he became a competent Major General during the Civil War, campaigning with Grant in his Western campaigns and with Sherman on his march through Georgia. Brady photo, courtesy Ansco Historical Collections.

NELLIE AND JESSE GRANT—The President's two youngest children. Brady photo, 1869, courtesy Ansco Historical Collections.

JULIA AND HER FATHER—Left to right: Julia Dent Grant, her daughter Nellie, her father Colonel Dent, and her son Jesse. Brady-Handy collection, 1868-1869, courtesy Library of Congress.

Chapter Thirteen

No Place for Generals

By the spring of 1871 considerable feeling had generated against Grant. The harsh contacts of politics had dulled the gloss of his military reputation. He had shown no more aptitude for politics than he had for tanning. Yet as his term drew to a close it became more evident that he would be his own successor.

There was general prosperity in the North, and the South was improving with the increasing production of cotton. The Treaty of Washington negotiated by Hamilton Fish, had obtained an award of $15,500,000 from the British for Civil War damage claims resulting from the British-built Confederate raider Alabama. Public credit had been maintained despite efforts to repudiate the public debt.

Early in 1872 the Liberal Republican Convention nominated New York newspaper editor Horace Greeley for President, and B. Gratz Brown of Missouri for Vice President. On July 9th at Baltimore these nominations were ratified at the Democratic National Convention in spite of Greeley's previous opposition to Democratic principles.

When the Republicans met at Philadelphia on June 5th they renominated Grant on the first ballot. Henry Wilson of Massachusetts was nominated for Vice President. The only issue would be whether the Grant Administration be approved.

Grant was credited with strengthening the country's financial credit, increasing American prestige abroad and using a firm hand to administer and enforce law both in the North and in the South. Against him was held the appointment of unworthy friends to positions they were unqualified for, and his excessive interference in Congressional affairs.

Again, Grant's Civil War reputation won him the election. On November 5, 1872, he won with a popular majority of 763,000, and an electoral college majority of 286 to 66.

On March 4, 1873, in his second inaugural address he said: "I did not ask for place or position, and was entirely without influence or the acquaintance of persons of influence, but was resolved to perform my part in a struggle threatening the very existence of the nation. I performed a conscientious duty, without asking promotion or command, and without a revengeful feeling toward any section or individual.

"Notwithstanding this, throughout the war, and from my candidacy for my present office in 1868 to the close of the last presidential campaign, I have been the subject of abuse and slander scarcely equaled in political history, which today I feel that I

RELAXATION AT LONG BRANCH, NEW JERSEY—Grant is shown with his family in front of his summer cottage which stood west of a long line of hotels at this resort area. Taken about 1870. Courtesy Chicago Historical Society.

can afford to disregard in view of your verdict, which I gratefully accept as my vindication."

The postwar boom and prosperity came to a sudden end on September 18, 1873. The disastrous panic began when once-sound financial institutions began to fail through overextension of credits. The treatment suggested to relieve the malady was printing more money. The bill introduced for this purpose at first seemed to be the solution, so Grant thought. After another hard look at the problem and the solution offered, he resolved to veto the Inflation Bill. His firm opposition against the bill culminated in the passage of a bill that limited inflation.

But with all his problems there were moments of happiness. On May 21, 1874 his only daughter Nellie was married in the White House to a young Englishman she had met on a transatlantic voyage some 18 months earlier. He was Algernon G. F. Sartoris, a nephew of the famous stage actress "Fanny" Frances Anne Kemble. And on October 20, 1874, his oldest son, Second Lieutenant Frederick Dent Grant, married Ida Honoré at her home in Chicago. Fred, while serving under Phil Sheridan in Chicago had met her at a social affair. Less than two years later, and while still attached to the Seventh Cavalry, he was saved from possible death with Custer and his command at the Little Big Horn, by being on leave at the White House for the birth of his first child Julia.

"Cump" Sherman as General-in-Chief never had

liked Washington. He had warned Grant about going there in 1864, advice he followed by moving down with George Meade. Secretary of War William W. Belknap had taken over the functions of commander-in-chief to a degree that Sherman asked for and received permission to establish army headquarters at St. Louis. He arrived there September 3rd.

A scandal broke when Secretary of the Treasury Benjamin H. Bristow uncovered a fraud in which a large group of distillers in collusion with government agents were permitting the sale of untaxed liquor. The Whisky Ring involved Grant's chief secretary, General Orville A. Babcock. Babcock had been taking large sums of money and expensive gifts, and Grant himself had accepted a valuable team of horses complete with harness though he was unaware of what had been transpiring. The same could not be said of Babcock.

When first confronted with the conspiracy Grant had said: "Let no guilty man escape." As the evidence became more conclusive, Babcock requested a court martial as a miiltary officer. He feared a civil court. When the court martial convened it was provided with a deposition from the President acting as a character witness in Babcock's behalf. This voluntary testimony of the President was so favorable no jury would have convicted him.

The Keokuk Packet Line and other steamboat people opposed the erection of the St. Louis bridge designed by Grant's friend Captain James B. Eads.

The Keokuk people had filed a complaint with Secretary Belknap who appointed a commission of army engineers. Testimony was accepted only from the steamboat people.

To the astonishment of the St. Louis community, the commission reported that though the bridge was consructed exactly according to the Act of Congress, it was an obstruction to navigation and should be removed or a ship canal built around it.

Captain Eads and Dr. Taussig, general manager of the Bridge Company, called on Grant. When Grant heard their case he summoned Belknap, who claimed authority to remove obstructions to navigation. Grant advised him that only Congress had that right and hardly would do it to save high smokestacks from having to be lowered. He concluded by advising Belknap to tell his Keokuk friends, if aggrieved, they could sue the bridge company for damages.

Heister Clymer, chairman of the House Committee on Expenditures in the War Department, discovered early in his investigation that Secretary Belknap was guilty of the sale of post traderships and other criminal acts. On March 2, 1876, his committee requested that impeachment proceedings be started. When this news reached Belknap he rushed over to Grant's office with his resignation. It was accepted immediately. Though Grant did not have any information other than that supplied by Belknap, he believed him innocent and shielded him accordingly. Grant's opponents, in making a political field day out of his stubborn adherence to his friend in disgrace, believed he covered himself with a film of suspicion.

The Senate began impeachment proceedings against Belknap for malfeasance in office. Failing to convict him for lack of a two-thirds vote, the majority that voted "no" believed him guilty but were convinced the Senate had no jurisdiction once the President had accepted the resignation.

Among the various witnesses ordered to appear before the committee was General George Armstrong Custer. Courageously daring to testify against one of Grant's pet appointees, Belknap, he incurred additional hatred by telling of some of the manipulations of post tradserships by the President's brother Orvil. Orvil had done all right for himself at a number of the western posts.

Custer could not return to his command at Fort Abraham Lincoln without permission. His testimony completed, he hoped to return in time to lead his troops against the Sioux. The President continued to delay him in Washington. Repeatedly, Custer attempted to see him to correct certain wrong impressions, but was refused an audience. By a prior agreement with Sherman, since he had been released by the committee, Custer left for Fort Lincoln.

Because Custer did not have an official authorization from the War Department to leave town, Grant took the opportunity to place him in arrest on his arrival in Chicago, and order him not to accompany the expedition.

Generals Sheridan, E. D. Townsend and Alfred Terry had requested executive clemency, while Custer had wired the President: "I appeal to you as a soldier to spare me the humiliation of seeing my regiment march to meet the enemy and I not to share its dangers."

It is not likely that Custer's appeal or that of the three generals caused Grant to relent. This was an election year and Grant had reason to believe he would be trying for a third term. The newspapers had always liked the colorful Custer who could fight and win without the aid of booze, for Custer was a teetotaler. When the vituperative

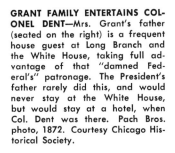

GRANT FAMILY ENTERTAINS COLONEL DENT—Mrs. Grant's father (seated on the right) is a frequent house guest at Long Branch and the White House, taking full advantage of that "damned Federal's" patronage. The President's father rarely did this, and would never stay at the White House, but would stay at a hotel, when Col. Dent was there. Pach Bros. photo, 1872. Courtesy Chicago Historical Society.

BY THE SEA—President and Mrs. Grant with son Jesse at Long Branch, 1872. From a stereo photograph, courtesy Chicago Historical Society.

CADET FREDERICK DENT GRANT—Entering West Point in 1866 at age 16 he graduated in 1871. Photo by Alexander Gardner about 1870, courtesy Chicago Historical Society.

press bore down on Grant's thin skin like a swarm of angry bees, he was vulnerable; so he permitted Custer to command the famous Seventh Cavalry in the Dakota column.

The *New York World* of May 2nd, under a heading *Grant's Revenge*, charged Grant with misusing his official power in relieving Custer of his command because he "gave important testimony . . . relative to the post tradership frauds." An editorial stated that though Custer's testimony was not voluntary and not disrespectful to the President, his removal would deter others who might testify in the future. On May 29, 1876, Grant released the announcement he would not be a candidate for a third term. It was clairvoyance.

The Custer tragedy on June 25, 1876, was exactly what the Democrats needed for the election campaign. *The New York Herald* asked, "Who Slew Custer?" then answered by indicating the Grant peace policy that fed and clothed the Indian families while the warriors were killing our troops —"that is what killed Custer . . . that nest of thieves, the Indian Bureau, with its thieving agents and favorites as Indian traders . . . that is what killed Custer. . . ."

The *New York Times* indicated that the administration, whatever its faults, attempted to treat the Indian fairly.

The *New York Herald*, on July 17th, left some questions unanswered by saying: "Had Sheridan been killed by the Indians instead of Custer, President Grant would have published an address on the subject. But for Custer, who made Sheridan,

and did more than any one man to make Grant President, the Sitting Bull of the White House has never a word to offer."

Even now it appears that Grant added little to his fame as a result of his eight years in office. His selection by the Republican party had been to save the party, not to reward or to honor him. He left office amidst an almost universal feeling that he was to blame for the. scandals of his administration. Seldom had he been able to resist the influence of men of wealth or prominence. Despite this he was an honest man. Senator John Sherman, who knew him well, stated: "General Grant was, in every sense of the word, an honest man. He was so honest that he did not suspect others, and no doubt confided in, and was friendly with, those who abused his confidence." Unfortunately he was unable to determine who was honest.

He had tried to do his best in his stubborn, determined way but it hadn't gone too well. A master at strategy but never good at tactics, he had discovered a good politician had to be a master at both. He was disgusted and sick of it all. In three more months he could do the thing he loved to do best—travel. To his son Jesse he had said: "We will start as soon as possible after my successor is installed. We will take whatever money there is and we will go far and stay as long as it lasts." He had wanted a trip around the world all of his life. He would soon be free to get his wish.

On December 5th, he gave Congress his last message. Summing up his years at the White House he recalled that:

GRANT'S LONG BRANCH COTTAGE—The summer White House for most of Grant's years as President. Pach Bros. photo. Courtesy Illinois State Historical Library.

PRESIDENT GRANT AND FRIENDS AT PULLMAN ISLAND—President Grant at right in rocking chair with back to camera. Mrs. Grant seated on step facing camera. 1872. Courtesy Chicago Historical Society.

"It was my fortune, or misfortune, to be called to the office of Chief Executive without any previous political training. . . . Under such circumstances it is but reasonable to suppose that errors of judgment must have occurred. Even had they not, differences of opinion between the Executive, bound by an oath to the strict performance of his duties, and writers and debaters must have arisen. It is not necessarily evidence of blunder on the part of the Executive because there are these differences of views. Mistakes have been made, as all can see and I admit . . . Failures have been errors of judgment, not of intent."

SILVER SIDEWALK OF CENTRAL CITY, COLORADO—April 29, 1873 President Grant was conducted to the Teller House (men on right are seated in front of its step) to find that "The sidewalk immediately fronting the entrance was paved with silver bricks to the value of 12 or 13 thousand dollars, sent over for that purpose by A. D. Breed of the Caribou Mine." Chas. S. Weitzle photo courtesy Denver Public Library Western Collection. Ca. 1870's.

JULIA SIMPSON GRANT—It appears as though Brady got a new carpet for this sitting. Ca. 1872. Courtesy Library of Congress.

A PARTY FOR THE PRESIDENT AT DR. TIFFANY'S COTTAGE—Oak Bluffs, Martha's Vineyard, 1874. From a stereo, courtesy Chicago Historical Society.

GRANT INAUGURATION IN 1873—Grant had discovered that a term as President was not without responsibilities though it had its compensations. In his inaugural address this March 4th he said: "I have been the subject of abuse and slander scarcely ever equaled in political history, which today I feel that I can afford to disregard in view of your verdict, which I gratefully accept as my vindication." Courtesy Library of Congress.

AN INCREDULOUS PRESIDENT—These thirty bars of silver kept Grant's feet clean and dry for he was the first President to set foot on Colorado. Man at left is metallurgist Richard Pearce. Man leaning with hand on door is Nathaniel P. Hill. This was the first smelter in Black Hawk, Colo. 1868. Courtesy Denver Public Library Western Collection.

THE PRICE OF POPULARITY—On October 16, 1873 during the reunion of the Army of the Tennessee held in Toledo, Ohio, a grand reception was held for the ladies at the Opera House. President Grant stood first in the reception line, Gen. Sherman second, Gen. Sheridan third, and Gen. Custer last. The dignity with which it began was altered when Phil Sheridan picked up a little girl and kissed her. Of course Gen. Custer followed suit, and soon Gen. Sherman and even Grant followed. Before long Sheridan kissed a young lady and the others, not to be outdone, followed suit. "The President blushed at the rashness of his young officers, but directly his eyes began to sparkle and he took out his handkerchief and wiped his mouth." According to the **Toledo Commercial**, 2,000 ladies shook hands with all four. Those kissed during the reception were as follows:

	Babies	Little Girls	Ladies
Grant	74	113	393
Sherman	127	147	297
Sheridan	94	104	410
Custer	83	138	417

Illustration from **Frank Leslie's Illustrated Newspaper**, Nov. 8, 1873.

THE THIRD TERM QUESTION—A cartoon in the **New York Daily Graphic**, October 24, 1874. Courtesy Chicago Historical Society.

INDIAN DELEGATION FROM DAKOTA—Seated, left to right: Sitting Bull, The Minor (Oglala); Swift Bear (Brule'); Spotted Tail (Brule'); Standing left to right: Julius Meyer, interpreter and trader; Red Cloud (Oglala). Grant had pressed the passage of the Act of March 3, 1871, providing that no Indian tribe or nation would be recognized thereafter as an independent power to deal with by treaty. This Indian delegation came to Washington to visit "The Great White Father," as they called him. Photo by Frank F. Currier, May, 1872. Courtesy The Smithsonian Institution.

A PRESIDENT AND A VICEROY OF CHINA MEET—Grant and Li Hung Chang became immediate friends thoroughly enjoying each others company. Photo taken in Tien Tsin, 1879. Courtesy Chicago Historical Society.

DELEGATION TO MEET PRESIDENT GRANT—This delegation was headed by Chief Spotted Tail (top row, center with # on his sleeve). Chief Sitting Bull, The Minor is immediately to the left of him. Chief Sitting Bull (Oglala) was presented with a Henry repeating rifle in a leather case by the Commissioner of Indian Affairs from President Grant on June 6, 1875 saying: "Your conduct has been reported to the President, and I am instructed to give you a token of his regard in recognition of your good services." May, 1875. Courtesy Col. Brice C. W. Custer.

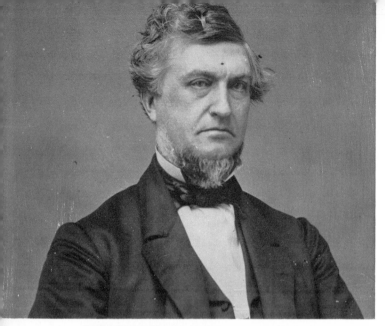

SENATOR ZACHARIAH CHANDLER OF DETROIT—He was appointed Secretary of the Interior in 1875 by Grant after he had been defeated by Supreme Court Justice Isaac P. Christiancy, a Democrat from Monroe. Chandler, who was a Radical Republican leader and against the mild policies of Lincoln and Johnson, though honestly was against civil service. He believed in political patronage to support himself and strengthen his party. Brady-Handy collection. Courtesy Library of Congress.

MRS. JULIA DENT GRANT—Taken while abroad about 1877, by Atelier Heliosy. Courtesy Ohio Historical Society.

PRESIDENT GRANT'S CABINET—1876-1877—Illustration from "Life of Zachariah Chandler," Detroit Post & Tribune Co. Courtesy Detroit Historical Museum.

BREECH PLATE ENGRAVING OF SITTING BULL'S RIFLE—This rifle was retrieved by Col. Nelson A. Miles following the murder of Sitting Bull by enemy Crow Indians on the Tongue River, Montana, in December, 1876. Photograph courtesy of Museum of The American Indian, Heye Foundation.

PRESIDENT GRANT PRESENTS SITTING BULL WITH A RIFLE—This was the Henry 15-shot .44 calibre rifle given to Tatanka Yotanka, better known as Sitting Bull The Good, for he was very friendly to the white man. The other Sitting Bull (Hunkpapa), 10 years older, was the noted opponent of Custer, and was not to meet Grant until 1883. Photograph courtesy of Museum of The American Indian, Heye Foundation.

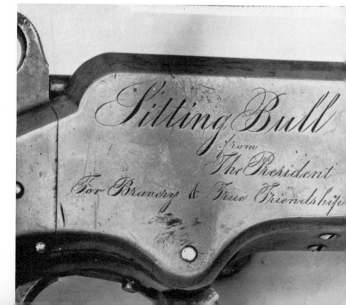

RETURN FROM WORLD TOUR—Grant arrived in San Francisco on the steamer "City of Tokio" in September of 1879. Escorted by a fleet of yachts he was saluted by guns from the forts as he passed the Golden Horn. Sketch in **Harpers Weekly**, October 25, 1879. Courtesy Denver Public Library Western Collection.

CANAL BUSINESS—**Puck Magazine** takes a poke at Grant. Keppler cartoon in the issue of September 17, 1879 during the period Grant's political friends were trying to whip up a third term storm in his favor. Courtesy Ohio Historical Society.

SALUTE ON THE SAND LOTS OF SAN FRANCISCO—It was a triumphal return for the old warrior. From photographs by Bradley and Rulofson. **Harper's Weekly**, October 25, 1879. Courtesy Denver Public Library Western Collection.

THE WATCH FOR GRANT—Enthusiasm for Grant was evident here on San Francisco's "Sand Lots" at it was everywhere else **he** visited. **Harper's Weekly**, October 25, 1879. Courtesy Denver Public Library Western Collection.

RECEPTION IN COURT OF THE PALACE HOTEL—No king received higher accord. **Harper's Weekly**, October 25, 1879. Courtesy Denver Public Library Western Collection.

RECEPTION IN SACRAMENTO—Grand procession honoring Grant on K Street as it appeared looking south from Third Street, October 22, 1879. From **The Mirror**, Nov. 8, 1879. Courtesy California State Library.

SACRAMENTO HOLDS A RECEPTION FOR MRS. GRANT—This friendly gesture honoring Mrs. Grant occurred in the Senate Chamber of the Capitol Building October 22, 1879. From **The Mirror**, Nov. 8, 1879. Courtesy California State Library.

ON A SEARCH FOR SILVER—President Grant and his party were guided through the Bonanza silver mine in Virginia City, Nevada, October 28, 1879, by the "two richest miners in the world," J. W. Mackay at extreme left and Col. J. G. Fair on extreme right. Grant bet Mackay a silver dollar Mrs. Grant would not go down the mine shaft. When she learned of his bet there was no hesitation on her part. Grant lost. Courtesy Chicago Historical Society.

CHICAGO PAYS ITS RESPECT—A wild, enthusiastic crowd greeted the Ex-President. Grant reviewed the parade from the Palmer House. Sketch by A. Berghaus in **Frank Leslie's Illustrated Newspaper**, November 22, 1879. Courtesy Chicago Historical Society.

GRANT'S RETURN TO MEXICO—After settling down at home Grant took his family on a visit to Mexico, a country in which he had a deep interest. This view of the valley of Mexico from Chapultepec was in **Harper's Weekly**, April 17, 1880. Courtesy Illinois State Historical Library.

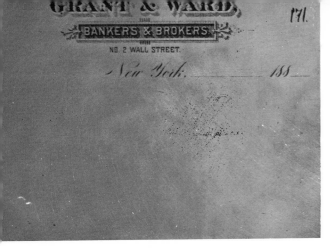

GRANT AND WARD LETTERHEAD—Courtesy Chicago Historical Society.

GUESTS IN SANTE FE, NEW MEXICO—The Grants with Mrs. Fred Grant and daughter on the porch of General G. A. Smith, July 10, 1880. Photo by Ben Wittick, Santa Fe. Courtesy State Historical Society of Colorado Library.

AN ENGLISH POLITICAL CARTOON—**Puck** took a great interest in American political trends and enjoyed editorializing. From **Puck,** January 1880. Courtesy The Ohio Historical Society.

BUCK GRANT—Ulysses S. Grant, Jr., who thought himself a financier, invited his father to become a partner in the Wall Street brokerage firm of Grant & Ward. Little did they know that this Wall Street wizard Ward had no crystal ball for he was a swindler. Ca. 1882. Courtesy The Ohio Historical Society.

GRANT FAMILY AT MT. McGREGOR—Seated left to right: Julia Grant (F. D. Grant's daughter), Mrs. U. S. Grant, U. S. Grant (third son of F. D. Grant), Gen. U. S. Grant, Nellie Grant (daughter of Jesse R. Grant): Standing, left to right: Mrs. Fred (Ida Honore) Grant, Col. Fred Grant, Mrs. Jesse (Elizabeth C.) Grant, Mrs. Nellie Grant Sartoris, U. S. Grant, Jr. (second son of U. S. Grant). Photo by W. H. Baker, Saratoga, June 19, 1885.

JAMES W. DREXEL COTTAGE AT MOUNT McGREGOR, NEW YORK— in the Adirondacks Mountains near Saratoga Springs, Grant spent his remaining days writing his **Memoirs**. He moved to this cottage of a friend of his on June 16, 1885 to avoid New York City's summer heat. Courtesy Chicago Historical Society.

LAST PICTURE OF GRANT WITH HIS FAMILY—Taken four days before his death, July 19, 1885. Left to right: General Grant, Mrs. U. S. Grant, Mrs. Nellie Grant Sartoris, Mrs. Fred Grant. Courtesy Library of Congress.

GRANT FAMILY AT MT. McGREGOR—Taken about July 10 by F. L. Howe of New York; the General had lost weight. Top row, left to right: Jesse R. Grant, General Grant, Mrs. U. S. Grant, Mrs. Jesse R. Grant, Col. Frederick D. Grant; Bottom row, left to right: Mrs. Nellie Grant Sartoris, Fred Grant's daughter Julia, Fred Grant's son Ulysses S., Jesse Grant's daughter Nellie, Mrs. Fred Grant. Courtesy Library of Congress

MARK TWAIN—Samuel L. Clemens, better known by his pen name Mark Twain, was a friend of General Grant. He offered Grant a check of $25,000 advance royalty for the first volume of his **Memoirs** and $25,000 royalty for each additional volume. Grant's 1,231 pages totaling 295,000 words brought his family nearly $450,000 within the first two years. Brady-Handy photo. Courtesy Library of Congress.

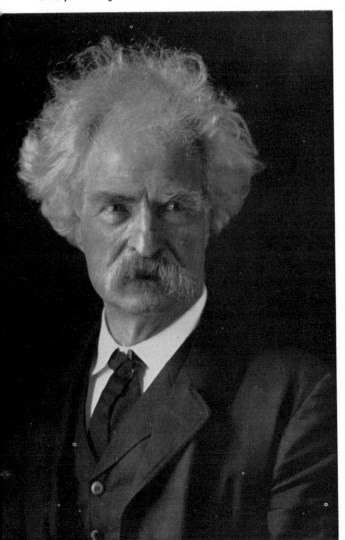

the cocaine has got to be very disagreeable. It has paralized and swollen my tongue in til my mouth will scarsely hold it. I take no more morphine in the twenty-four hours because I take three minims (drops) in

the day time. That is simply left off of what I take at night. It has not been taken but once. It will only be taken when I am a great sufferer. It will be a good thing if I can keep my head until I have recovered my strength partially.

GRANT KEPT DR. DOUGLAS INFORMED—Since he could not talk during his last days Grant wrote notes; these notes to keep his physician informed as to his reaction to the opiates administered for the relief of his pain. Courtesy Chicago Historical Society.

MEDICAL REPORT OF GRANT'S PHYSICIANS—Drs. John Hancock Douglas and George F. Shrady sign a consultation record, probably in April of 1885. Courtesy Chicago Historical Society.

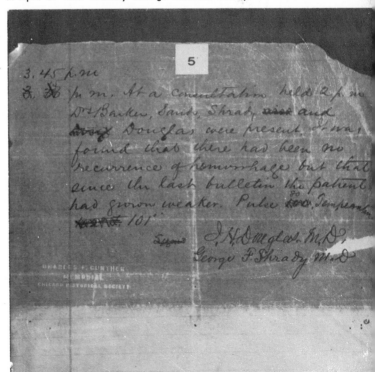

The death of General U. [S] Grant, late President of th[e] United States, is an event tha[t] must elicit the profoundest e[x] pression of sorrow from a grat[e] ful people. The unselfish dev[o] tion to his country, the grea[t] services rendered by him, (whic[h] were recognized by the entir[e] world,) render appropriate som[e] public manifestation of the un[i] versal feeling.

I therefore request the peop[le] of Marion to meet at the CIT[Y] HALL this Thursday Evening at 8 o'clock, for the purpos[e] above indicated.

C. P. GAILEY,
Mayor.

July 23d, 1885.

AN ENTIRE NATION MOURNED—Appropriate proclamations were offered by mayors in cities large and small. Mayor Gailey of Marion, Ohio, displays a universal expression. Courtesy The Ohio Historical Society.

THE GRANT TOMB—RIVERSIDE PARK, NEW YORK CITY—With the ground broken April 27, 1891, the tomb was dedicated April 27, 1897. Photo shows tomb while under construction about 1896. Courtesy The National Park Service.

DEATH OF GENERAL GRANT—Currier & Ives lithograph, 1885. Courtesy Library of Congress.

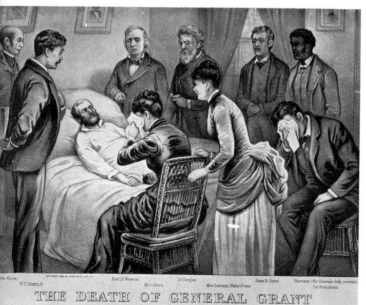

THE DEATH OF GENERAL GRANT
AT MOUNT MC. GREGOR, SARATOGA CO. NEW YORK, JULY 23RD 1885.

Chapter Fourteen

Rolling Stone

When the question of a third term arose and Grant had rejected the idea, General Sherman announced he was in favor of the governor of his home state, Rutherford B. Hayes of Ohio. The big question was "Whom will Grant support?" With Grant's support, Hayes easily took the nomination from James G. Blaine.

Grant's second term had drawn to a close on March 4, 1877, when he appeared to see Hayes sworn in. Now a private citizen with $25,000 in cash, he was ready to travel with Julia and his 19 year old son Jesse.

While in Philadelphia the week before they sailed, the Grants were the guests of George W. Childs. Philadelphians vied with each other to fete and honor him before he embarked on his voyage around the world. All of a sudden things were right. Newspapers that had been hurling vehement and scathing remarks at him suddenly became benevolent in their complimentary remarks and well wishing.

Sailing from Philadelphia on May 17th, the *Indiana* arrived in Liverpool, England, eleven days later. Though the press had hardly mentioned his arrival, 10,000 people were present to greet him.

In London there was some question of protocol. How was an ex-president to be received by the Queen who had invited his family to visit her at Windsor Castle for dinner on June 27th and to remain as overnight guests? It was Adam Badeau who obtained the decision that the British Government would receive him as an ex-sovereign.

In his responses Grant would humbly and modestly state he knew the honor bestowed upon him was intended for America as much as for himself. The great enthusiasm evident in England and every country he visited indicated they considered him a great military leader.

Taking the summer on the continent, he returned to travel that fall through England and Scotland. The winter was spent on a Mediterranean cruise on the *Vandalia*, returning to Paris for the opening of the Paris Exhibition May 7, 1878.

In Berlin Prince Bismarck welcomed him at his Radziwill Palace with extended hands. They took an instant liking to each other. One of Bismarck's first questions was about Sheridan, who had campaigned with him in France. They had become great friends, the prince making the observation that Sheridan seemed to be a man of great ability. "Yes," said Grant, "I regard Sheridan as not only one of the great soldiers of our war, but one of the great soldiers of the

HIRAM ULYSSES GRANT—Was his name about one month after birth. At West Point on Roe's Hotel guest book he signed as "Ulysses H. Grant." Later, on the Adjutant's register, he signed "Ulysses Hiram Grant." By an error his appointment papers had been made for "Ulysses Simpson Grant." He would have been refused admission under any other name, so he adopted it. This engraving, from his first photo, was taken in Cincinnati during the summer of 1843, at age 21. Just out of West Point, he was a brevet Second Lieutenant assigned to the Fourth Infantry. Courtesy Library of Congress.

Lieut. U. S. Grant at

LIEUTENANT GRANT—From a Daguerreotype taken while stationed at Sacketts Harbor, N. Y. in 1849. The clean-shaven but long-haired 27 year-old newlywed lived in cramped quarters at Madison Barracks until spring with Julia, then moved to Detroit. Courtesy The Ohio Historical Society.

world—as a man who is fit for the highest commands. No better general ever lived than Sheridan." Grant and Bismarck met several times, each being delighted with the other's company.

Following a visit to the low countries, then Russia, the party passed through the Suez Canal on the steamer *Venetia* in January, 1879, for India.

In China, a warm friendship developed with Viceroy Li Hung Chang. Both were of the same age, 57. Chang thought it funny that his name was Li, and Grant's opponent was named Lee.

At the conclusion of his two years and four months of travel, Grant was of the opinion that the four greatest diplomats and statesmen in the world were Viceroy Li Hung Chang, Prince Bismarck, Leon Michel Gambetta and Lord Beaconfield.

The Administration under President Hayes had many questioning the outcome for the Republican party in 1880. The "old guard" had been reading of Grant's reception abroad and began to get ideas. They advised him to remain abroad until June of

1880; then his tour from California east could be used to great political advantage just before the party convention. The enthusiatic welcome he would receive at the last moment would make him appear as the obvious candidate and insure his nomination.

Time had softened his views toward politics and politicians. Julia had been softened, too, but her interest was her husband's interest. Julia was eager to return to the White House.

They arrived in San Francisco from Tokyo on September 20, 1879. His reception there and everywhere across the country was like that of a conquering hero. The acclamation, the orations, the huge crowds cheering and applauding, were manifestations of his popularity.

He had said he did not seek or wish a third term and would not accept the nomination except on one condition—"if social or public affairs at home would render it necessary . . . to go back as a military leader." At the time there had been some bloody and violent riots on the railroads that had created a state of public concern.

Having served two terms, he knew "the care, the responsibility, the abuse, the ingratitude attending the holding of office," and had never been as happy in his life as the day he left the White House. Disregarding his indifference to renomination, his political friends appealed to his deep sense of patriotism and his indebtedness to his party. He could not conscientiously refuse.

The Republican National Convention was held in Chicago June 2, 1880. Grant's campaign man-

ager, Roscoe Conklin of New York, believed he would have Grant nominated on the first ballot if the unit rule prevailed. The state goes as the majority of its delegates when on the unit rule.

Three things went against Grant. The convention wouldn't adopt the unit rule; Elihu Washburne got himself nominated, and John Sherman was nominated. All three factors took votes from Grant. On the first ballot Grant received 304 against James G. Blaine's 284. On the 35th ballot it was Grant 313, Blaine 257, Sherman 99 and Garfield 50. 378 votes were needed for nomination. It was a deadlock only a trade could break.

Sherman's managers offered to throw in his votes if Grant would appoint him Secretary of the Treasury. When Grant was approached for his reaction, he said: "It was my intention, if nominated

BRIGADIER GENERAL U. S. GRANT—Captain Grant's resignation from the army was accepted by Secretary of War Jefferson Davis on June 2, 1854. Grant was appointed Colonel of the Twenty-First Regiment of Illinois Volunteers by Governor Richard Yates, June 15, 1861. President Lincoln nominated him a Brigadier General "to rank as such from the seventeenth day of May, 1861." Photo was taken at Cairo, Ill., October 1861. Courtesy Library of Congress.

MISTER SAM GRANT, REALTOR—Appearing hard and businesslike, Grant was soft-as-mush when it came to collecting rent in St. Louis. It was this year of 1859 he "set free forever" his negro slave William Jones. Courtesy Missouri Historical Society.

and elected, to appoint John Sherman Secretary of the Treasury. Now you may be certain that I shall not. Not to be President of the United States would I consent that a bargain be made."

On the 36th ballot Garfield received 399 votes to Grant's 306. Blaine had turned the trick for it was his work behind the scenes that broke the deadlock. Garfield did not receive a letter or telegram of congratulations from Grant, though before the summer was over he was called upon by him. Grant's friends had let him down.

SWORD AND SASH POSE—Grant rarely carried a sword, and then only for dress occasions. Photograph was taken by J. W. Campbell, photographer with the 20th Army Corps, Army of the Cumberland, at a camp at Chattanooga in late 1863. Courtesy Chicago Historical Society.

The time had arrived to consider what to do for a living. He had about $100,000 that brought him a return of about $5,000 a year—enough to live on in Galena but not enough for New York.

His friends had an idea. George W. Jones, publisher of the *New York Times*, promoted a trust fund for Grant and his family to be administered by Jay Gould, John W. Mackay, William H. Vanderbilt and the *Times*, each contributing $25,000. A total of $250,000 was raised by popular subscription which, when invested, gave the Grants an income of $15,000 annually.

In the spring of 1881, Grant made a trip to Mexico after which he became president of Jay Gould's Mexican Southern Railroad. His major interest was a railroad between the United States and Mexico.

That August he purchased a brownstone home at 3 East 66th Street in New York City. This permitted him to be near his son Ulysses Jr., who had married the daughter of the wealthy Hon. Jerome B. Chaffee and conducted a business on Wall Street. Jesse was just out of the Columbia Law School, while Fred was a lieutenant colonel in the army.

NEW COAT FOR THE GENERAL—Late in 1862, before the Vicksburg campaign began, the noted Civil War photographer Mathew B. Brady, took this picture of Grant before his new uniform got its usual "used" look. Promotion to the rank of major general, on February 17th, was reason enough for a new coat. Courtesy Ansco Historical Collection.

Ulysses Jr., otherwise known as Buck, had gone into a Wall Street partnership with a young man by the name of Ferdinand Ward.

Both Buck and his father had put $100,000 each in the new banking and brokerage firm. Neither questioned why or how they managed to receive two or three thousand dollars a month on their investment. Ward had said he had his money tied up in large corporations so would match their investment with $200,000 in high grade stocks and bonds. The two Grants were dupes enough to believe his story.

Ward was a typical con man playing on human avarice. He used the ex-President's name to great advantage in getting veterans and millionaires to leave money with him for investment, paying them large dividends from imagined earnings on his investments which actually were sums of money some more recent victim had paid him to invest. In turn he would take the moneys obtained and play the stock market with abandon, invariably losing. It was just a matter of time.

On May 6, 1884, the firm of Grant and Ward collapsed. When the swindle was fully exposed in the courts, the liabilities of the firm were over 16 million dollars with assets of but 67 thousand dollars. Ward had kept two sets of books, one of which was his secret set. For his reward he received ten years in the state penitentiary.

Grant was criticized by many papers, some accusing him of benefiting by the swindling. There is no question that he was innocent of what was going on about him. He had lost all of his money, even having to sell his wife's houses in Washington and the Dent property near St. Louis.

But there was more to come. He had trusted when others had withdrawn their trust. There remained his $250,000 trust fund, the interest from which would keep them quite comfortably. Suddenly it ceased to provide income. It was entirely invested in railroad stock, and the railroads existed no longer. Grant's trust in man ran out.

Needing a rest, the Grants spent the summer of 1884 at Long Beach, New Jersey. It was at this time he discovered that the eating of peaches irritated his throat. Near the end of the summer Dr. Da Costa, a Philadelphia throat specialist, while paying him a call, examined his throat and then urged him to see someone in New York. He disregarded the advice until his throat pains caused Mrs. Grant to insist on seeing Dr. Fordyce Barker, who advised immediate consultation that same day of October 22nd with Dr. John H. Douglas. Douglas frankly told him it was a condition with a cancerous

NO SWORDSMAN HERE—Major General Grant disliked to wear or use arms. Photographs of him wearing a sword are rare. Taken by Bishop, photographer with the Army of the Cumberland, presumably in early 1864. Courtesy Chicago Historical Society.

tendency, a conclusion Grant had reached previously.

He recalled an offer from *Century Magazine* to give him $500 each for a series of three articles on the Civil War. Though he had rejected the original offer at a time when he was not in want, conditions had changed. Samuel L. Clemens (Mark Twain), learning of this in November, 1884, visited the General at his 66th Street home. Grant told him of his desire to write his *Memoirs* for which the Century people would pay him 10 per cent royalty with no guarantee.

Clemens was aghast. He knew the Century people were honest but outrageously low in their estimate of the magic of the Grant name. He proposed to Grant that he would publish his *Memoirs*, paying him 20 per cent royalty and advancing him $25,000. The offer was accepted.

Grant began his dictation to a stenographer, Noble E. Dawson, on February 21, 1885. After several months his voice failed and it became extremely painful to whisper. A biopsy had revealed the dreaded, incurable malignancy. It would be a race to finish the proposed two volumes before death.

Sitting with a writing board on his lap, he would average four hours a day as he fought back the pain, to complete a legacy of financial security for his beloved family.

On June 16th he moved to a cottage at Mount McGregor, New York, to avoid the oppressing summer heat of New York City. It was owned by his friend James W. Drexel and was located near Saratoga Springs in the Adirondacks. Here he completed his manuscript a week before his death on July 23rd. Courageously, he had fought a last desperate battle and won, so that he might provide his family with security.

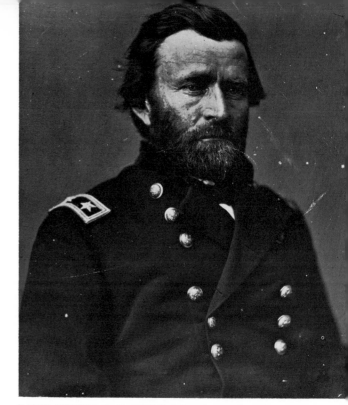

MAJOR GENERAL U. S. GRANT—Taken by Brady in late 1862. Courtesy Ansco Historical Collection.

GENERAL-IN-CHIEF—Taking command of all Federal armies March 12, 1864, Grant made his headquarters with the Army of the Potomac, to be near General Lee. Brady photo, courtesy Ansco Historical Collection.

LIEUTENANT GENERAL U. S. GRANT—Had his rank confirmed on March 2, 1864. A bill to restore the rank of lieutenant general had become a law on February 26, 1864, having been passed with the understanding Grant would be the man selected by President Lincoln. From this time on Grant resorted to an open coat and vest policy. Informal attire suited him best. Courtesy Chicago Historical Society.

AT CITY POINT, VIRGINIA—Lt. Gen. Grant adopted City Point for his headquarters in June of 1864. This photo taken there in early 1865 shows him wearing a look of determination. The unmilitary shirt he wears is a reflection of other unwarlike characteristics. He sickened at the sight of blood, and could not inflict pain. Courtesy Chicago Historical Society.

SIGNS OF STRAIN—In the autumn of 1864 the terrible drain of responsibility had begun to show. Earlier pictures show an unfurrowed forehead, a relaxed brow. Earlier, he had thought the war would be of short duration. Now he knew that it would take a lot of pounding to end it all. Brady photo, courtesy Ansco Historical Collection.

CARTE DE VISITE—Photographs on cards 2 1/2"x4" became extremely popular during the Civil War. Small and cheap (four for a dollar), they could be carried easily or mailed. Photographers made a big business of selling likenesses of popular military heroes. Photo by Alexander Gardner, ca. 1864-65, photographer to the Army of the Potomac. Courtesy Illinois State Historical Library.

AFTER APPOMATTOX—The tender-hearted general believed that, since more men died in camp from disease than from wounds, the quicker he could end the war, the more men would be saved. The hardest blows would bring the quickest results. Photo in 1865, courtesy The National Archives.

RELAXATION—With a fratricidal war now over and time to rest, give him a good cigar and a chair with armrests, and the result is a fine portrait. An unbuttoned coat and vest is characteristic of Grant's disdain for formality. Ca. 1865. Courtesy Chicago Historical Society.

PORTRAIT AT WEST POINT—Painted by Paul Louvier in 1866, this portrait of Lieutenant General Grant may be seen in the Library of the United States Military Academy. Courtesy The United States Military Academy Archives.

OUR FIRST FOUR-STAR GENERAL—Commissioned so on July 25, 1866, Grant retained his four-star rank until March 4, 1869, when he became President. He was re-appointed General, March 3, 1885, on the retired list, at the age of 63. Photo by Brady, 1866, courtesy Chicago Historical Society.

NO MUSIC LOVER—Grant was tone deaf. Though he could not distinguish one tune from another, he thought he could recognize "Hail to the Chief," it was played for him so often. If it was changed to "Yankee Doodle," he didn't know the difference. 1865. Courtesy Chicago Historical Society.

SECRETARY OF WAR ad interim—Secretary of War Stanton, a holdover from the Lincoln administration, refused to resign at President Johnson's request. Johnson ordered Grant to be Secretary of War temporarily, beginning August 12, 1867. When Congress insisted on Stanton's reinstatement, Grant resigned January 14, 1868. When Johnson accused him of a breach of faith, Grant never spoke to him again. Jeremiah Gurney photo, about 1868, courtesy Chicago Historical Society.

THE CHIEF SHOWS NO CHANGE—Though general of the armies of the United States, Grant continued to be careless of dress. He employed no small talk, either in public or in private. His speech was extremely rapid and in clear, terse sentences. His statements, like his military orders, were matter-of-fact. Brady photo, 1867, courtesy Library of Congress.

A CHILD IN POLITICS—Grant had no real exposure to politics prior to Appomattox. He had never seen a legislative body in action—had no conception how it functioned. Brady photo about 1870, courtesy National Archives.

"LET US HAVE PEACE"—Was the campaign slogan for the Republican campaign when Grant was nominated for President at Chicago, May 21, 1868. This slogan was the concluding line in Grant's letter of acceptance. This photo made by an unknown photographer about 1869 was Grant's favorite. Courtesy Chicago Historical Society.

PRESIDENT GRANT—March 4, 1869, was Inauguration Day for U.S. Grant. In his address, he said: "The office has come to me unsought; I commence its duties untrammeled. I bring to it a conscious desire and determination to fill it to the best of my ability to the satisfaction of the people." Brady photo, about 1871, Courtesy Library of Congress.

ALGER STORY—From clerk to the Presidency in eight years, is an unparalleled story of success. Henry Ward Beecher said: "Grant was available and lucky." This may be true though Grant believed that officers never were candidates for anything, never got elected to anything and never asked favors of politicians. Brady photo, about 1872, courtesy Ansco Historical Collection.

PROFILE OF A PRESIDENT—Unusual left profile of Grant with side whiskers was made expressly for his wife. He shaved his mustache and chinbeard so that his likeness might be cut on a cameo. Photo by Walker, June 2, 1875, courtesy National Archives.

DECEIVED BY FRIENDS—Grant was naive and unsophisticated when it came to the appointment of staff members in the army and in the White House. He was equally so in choosing his friends and business associates. Though he could not believe that trusted friends might deceive him, when asked what distressed him most in politics, he replied, "To be deceived by those I trusted." Brand photo, Chicago, about 1874, courtesy Chicago Historical Society.

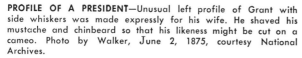

TRIP AROUND THE WORLD—Grant soon acquired the art of putting several appropriate thoughts together for various occasions. His statements were timely, modest, short and graceful. He maintained his dignity and humility by saying that the compliments given him were not meant for him but for his country. Photo by Taber, San Francisco, 1879. Courtesy Chicago Historical Society.

A FRIEND TO ALL—Horace Porter said of Grant: "Loyalty to his family, his friends, his country and his God so dominated his nature it sometimes led him into errors and caused him to stand by friends who were no longer worthy." Photo by Noe & Lee, Virginia City, Nevada, 1879, courtesy Chicago Historical Society.

UNUSUAL CHARACTER—In his earlier years of military life, Grant obtained relief from stressful situations by indulging in alcohol. His occasional excesses were of great concern to his family and friends, and of use to his detractors. There is no evidence that he abused its use in his presidential and later years or his critics would have made note of it. Brand photo, Chicago, about 1876, courtesy Chicago Historical Society.

GRANT LIKED TO LISTEN—A good listener, quickly grasping an idea and sifting out the facts, he brought them to a conclusion he seldom reversed. Bradley and Rulofson photo, San Francisco, 1879. Courtesy The Ohio Historical Society.

WALL STREET BUSINESSMAN—Offered a partnership in the investment firm of Grant & Ward, he accepted. Contributing both his money and his name, he sat back for the huge profits. Four years later the Wall Street wizard and con man Ward had absconded with all the funds leaving Grant and his friends penniless. 1881. Courtesy Library of Congress.

RETURN TO GALENA—Greater poise and an inner calm is evident in the former President as he revisits his Galena home. Photo by Lambertson & James, Galena, 1880. Courtesy Illinois State Historical Library.

GRANT ABOUT 1882—He smoked hardest when deep in thought. It aided his thinking and calmed his nervousness. On an average day he would smoke 12 rank, black cigars cutting down to two or three mild ones by 1884. Photographer unknown. Courtesy Galena Historical Society.

CITIZEN GRANT—This Brady photo was taken about 1883. With time on his hands he had ample opportunity to indulge in his walks about the city. Courtesy Library of Congress.

MR. PRESIDENT—Though Grant lacked the political acumen and experience while in office to accomplish his wishes, many of his policies were sound. He promoted civil service and economy in government; he favored payment of the public debt; he established a firm relationship with England and promoted good will with Mexico; and he improved conditions for the Indian. Photo by W. Kurtz, New York, 1884. Courtesy Galena Historical Society.

TENDERHEARTED GENERAL—As a boy Grant disliked hunting since it meant injuring a gamebird or animal, and the sight of blood sickened him. Perhaps this explains why he refused to eat game or fowl, preferring beef but only if welldone. He was fond of pork and beans, corn, cucumbers, and buckwheat cakes. Photo by John Carbutt, Chicago, probably early 1863. Courtesy Chicago Historical Society.

NEAR THE END—Valiantly Grant fought to stay alive so that he might complete his **Memoirs** and provide an adequate estate for his family. In his gradually weakening condition he worked long hours without complaint, completing his manuscript one week before his death. Photo by Gilman, Mt. McGregor, N.Y. four days before his death on July 23, 1885.

WRITING HIS MEMOIRS—Pressed financially after losing everything in the Grant & Ward swindle, Grant wrote three articles for Century Magazine receiving $500 each and a $1,500 bonus. Mark Twain offered him a $25,000 guarantee and 20% in royalties for his **Memoirs**. Grant began dictating in June, 1884. By fall his voice gave out from a malignancy of the tongue, so he resorted to writing the balance as he is seen doing here on the porch of a cottage at Mt. McGregor, New York, June 27, 1885. Courtesy Library of Congress.

STATUE OF U. S. GRANT IN PHILADELPHIA—This equestrian bronze statue of Grant by Daniel French and Edward Potter in Fairmount Park. Courtesy Philadelphia Fairmount Park Commission.

GENERAL GRANT STATUE IN CHICAGO—This equestrian monument by Louis T. Rebisso was unveiled October 7, 1891 in Lincoln Park. Photo by Marty Schmidt courtesy Chicago Historical Society. Statues of Grant have been erected across the nation.

GRANT EQUESTRIAN STATUE IN WASHINGTON, D. C.—Part of a large memorial to General Grant in which he faces the Mall in back of the Capitol Building. Courtesy Abbie Rowe, National Park Service, U. S. Department of Interior.

WORKING MODEL FOR GRANT MONUMENT AT VICKSBURG—Statue by Frederick C. Hibbard in 1917-1918. Courtesy Chicago Historical Society.

Acknowledgments

A book of this nature is not the work of one person. Fortunate am I to have assistance from so many kind people. Though I have given specific acknowledgments to institutions in the legend under the illustrations, there were many individuals who contributed in various ways. I am particularly indebted to:

Mrs. Francis Rhymer, curator of prints, Chicago Historical Society, for valuable assistance in selecting photographs.

Col. Vincent James Adduci, A.A.F. (retired) for direction and advice.

Mrs. Mildred Daiker, print and photo division, Library of Congress, for directing me into time-saving channels.

Kenneth W. Rapp, archivist, U. S. Military Academy, for his suggestions and direction into his resources many times.

Mrs. Vera Millhouse, Galena Historical Society, for direction and research.

Mrs. Elizabeth R. Martin, librarian, Ohio State Historical Society, for her many kindnesses and assistance.

Mrs. Alys Freeze, head, Denver Public Library Western Collection, for her assistance and suggestions.

Margot Pearsall, curator, department of social history, Detroit Historical Museum, whose knowledge of Grant while stationed in Detroit was a valued source of information.

Louis Torres, supervisory historian, National Park Service, New York City, for his leads on material and his fine suggestions on photographs.

Dr. R. Gerald McMurtry and his assistant Mrs. Ruth P. Higgins, Lincoln National Life Foundation, Fort Wayne, Indiana, for authoritative information and photographs.

Mrs. Mildred Schulz, reference librarian, and Margaret Flint, manuscript division, Illinois State Historical Library, for their many kindnesses and great aid.

Col. Brice C. W. Custer, U. S. A. (retired) for permission to use photographs from Mrs. E. B. Custer's collection.

Rachel Minick, curator of prints, New York Historical Society Library, for her painstaking assistance in my quest for Grant photographs.

Mrs. G. Stanley Smith, Sackets Harbor, N. Y., for the loan of valuable photographs.

May E. Fawcett, chief, audio-visual branch, and Elmer O. Parker, Army and Air Corps branch, National Archives, for repeated assistance and research.

Will Hellerman, Nationwide Insurance Co., Columbus, Ohio, for material from their famous print collection.

Richard S. Hagen, historian, Illinois State Department of Conservation, for suggestion that proved quite valuable.

Florence Ames, M. D., Monroe, Michigan, for her industrious pursuit of elusive Grant prints.

Major General U. S. Grant III, Washington, D. C., for his viewpoint on several matters.

Lawrence C. Hadley, chief of information, and Robert M. Utley, chief, historical studies division, National Park Service, Washington, D. C., for direction and suggestions.

Col. Frederick P. Todd, director, West Point Museum, for his great assistance in the procurement of illustrations.

Mrs. Dorothy Neuman, chief, Art Department, St. Louis Public Library, for assistance and a host of useful suggestions.

Henry Grunthal, assistant to the chief curator, American Numismatic Society Museum, New York City, for kindliness and information regarding the Grant medals and political pins.

Dr. Thomas M. Pitkin, historian (retired) National Park Service, New York City, for giving me early direction when it was needed most, for it saved considerable time.

The staffs of the Monroe County Library, Dorsch Memorial Library of Monroe, Detroit Public Library, Michigan State Library, Toledo Public Library and the Burton Historical Collections of Detroit, willingly obtained anything within their power to aid me. This alone was an invaluable assistance.

Mrs. Martha Barker, director, and Mrs. Raymond Pyle, curator, Monroe County Historical Museum, for their counsel and encouragement.

Robert J. Ege, Great Falls, Montana, for certain Grant letters.

Dr. Paul Mahaffey, Springfield, Ill.; Everett Sutton, Benkelman, Nebr.; Frank Mercatante, Grand Rapids, Mich.; Arthur Lesow, Monroe, Mich.; James R. Ketchum, curator of the White House Collection; Doris D. Walters, Hay Memorial Library, and Sallie Bohl, Sackets Harbor, N. Y.; Joseph B. Zywicki, Museum curator, and Archie Motley, manuscript division, Chicago Historical Commission; James McDaniel, Brookville, Pa., all of whom helped me in many ways.

William F. Kelleher, Cliffside Park, N. J., who searched diligently for materials and gave me continuous encouragement.

Mrs. Irene McCreery, local history department, Toledo Public Library, for many kindnesses and assistance.

Roy Hamlin, Monroe, Michigan, for his critical reading of my manuscript, his kindly and very constructive criticisms, and his assistance over my verbal morasses.

Senator Philip Hart of Michigan for his considerate assistance.

Dr. John Y. Simon, executive director, Ulysses S. Grant association, Carbondale, Illinois, who read and criticized my manuscript ably. Though he is in no way accountable for any errors, since I took issue with him on a few minor points and have not shown him my corrections on the others he had indicated, I deeply appreciate the time and thought this well-known Grant scholar has proffered me.

Mrs. Harriet Jennette, better known as Friday, who used her leisure time typing the entire manuscript—all this in addition to her many duties as my office assistant.

My wife Ethel for typing the bibliography and reading the entire manuscript several times for errors. Cheerfully she accepted the full occupation of my spare moments, even chaperoning me on several trips into Grant country.

L.A.F.

Bibliography

The following works have been read in the preparation of this volume.

ALLEN, WILLIAM H., *The American Civil War Book and Grant Album.* Boston, 1894.

ANDREWS, BENJAMIN E., *The United States in Our Time.* New York, 1903.

ANDREWS, J. CUTLER, *The North Reports the Civil War.* Pittsburg, 1955.

BADEAU, ADAM, *Grant In Peace.* Hartford, 1887.

BADEAU, ADAM, *Military History of Ulysses S. Grant.* 3 Vols., New York, 1881.

BEARSS, EDWIN C., *The Fall of Fort Henry.* West Tennessee Historical Society, Vol. 17, 1963.

BEARSS, EDWIN C., *Unconditional Surrender: The Fall of Fort Donaldson.* Tennessee Historical Quarterly, Vol. 21, Nos. 1 and 2, March, June, 1962.

BLACKFORD, SUSAN L., *Letters From Lee's Army.* New York, 1947.

BLACKWOOD, EMMA J., *To Mexico With Scott.* Cambridge, 1917.

BLAINE, JAMES G., *Twenty Years in Congress.* 2 Vols. Norwich, Conn., 1884.

BLAY, JOHN S., *The Civil War.* New York, 1958.

BOWERS, CLAUDE G., *The Tragic Era.* Cambridge, 1929.

BROWNING, ORVILLE H., *Diary of Orville Hickman Browning.* 3 Vols. Springfield, 1933.

BRYAN, JAMES, W., *The Grant Memorial in Washington.* Washington, D.C., 1924.

CATTON, BRUCE, *U. S. Grant and the American Military Tradition.* New York, 1954.

CHURCH, WILLIAM C., *Ulysses S. Grant and the Period of National Preservation and Reconstruction.* New York, 1897.

Civil War Times. April, May, June, Aug., Sept., Oct., Nov., 1960; Jan., Feb., Mar., 1961; Oct., 1964; Jan., Feb., Apr., 1965.

CLARKE, NORMAN E., SR., (editor) *Warfare Along the Mississippi.* Mount Pleasant, Mich., 1961.

CLEMENS, SAMUEL, *Mark Twain's Autobiography.* 2 Vols. New York, 1924.

COOLIDGE, LOUIS A., *Ulysses S. Grant.* Boston, 1917.

CRAMER, M. J., *Ulysses S. Grant: Conversations and Unpublished Letters.* New York, 1897.

CRAWFORD, T. C., *General Grant's Greatest Year.* McClure's Magazine, May, 1894.

CULLUM, GEORGE W., *Biographical Register of the Officers and Graduates of the U. S. Military Academy.* 3 Vols. New York, 1879.

CURRY, J. L. M., *The Peabody Education Fund.* Cambridge, 1898.

Daily Central City Register. Central City, Colo., April 26, 1873.

Daily Register-Call. Central City, Colo., July 29, 1880.

DANA, CHARLES A., *Recollections of the Civil War.* New York, 1898.

DANA, CHARLES A., and WILSON, J. H., *The Life of Ulysses S. Grant.* Chicago, 1868.

Detroit Post and Tribune, Zachariah Chandler. Detroit, 1880.

Dictionary of American Biography.

DODGE, THEODORE A., *A Bird's Eye View of the Civil War.* New York, 1897.

FARLEY, JOSEPH PEARSON, *West Point in the Early Sixties.* Troy, N.Y., 1902.

FORSYTH, GEORGE A., *Thrilling Days in Army Life.* New York, 1900.

FRANKLIN, JOHN HOPE, *Reconstruction after the Civil War.* Chicago, 1961.

FREEMAN, DOUGLAS S., *Lee's Lieutenants.* 3 Vols., New York, 1944.

FULLER, J. F. C., *Grant and Lee.* Bloomington, Ind., 1957.

GARLAND, HAMLIN, *Ulysses S. Grant: His Life and Character.* New York, 1898.

GORDON, JOHN B., *Reminiscences of the Civil War.* New York, 1903.

GRANT, JESSE R., *In the Days of My Father, General Grant.* New York, 1925.

GRANT, ULYSSES S., *Personal Memoirs of U.S. Grant.* 2 Vols. New York, 1895.

GREEN, HORACE, *General Grant's Last Stand.* New York, 1936.

GREENE, LAURANCE, *America Goes to Press.* Indianapolis, 1936.

GRODINSKY, JULIUS, *Jay Gould—His Business Career.* Philadelphia, 1957.

HANCOCK, MRS. W. S., *Reminiscences of Winfield Scott Hancock.* New York, 1887.

HARRIS, WILMER C., *Public Life of Zachariah Chandler.* Lansing, 1917.

HASKELL, JOHN, *The Haskell Memoirs.* New York, 1960.

HERGESHEIMER, JOSEPH, *Sheridan: A Military Narrative.* New York, 1931.

HESSELTINE, WILLIAM B., *Ulysses S. Grant: Politician.* New York, 1935.

HOLLISTER, O. J., *Life of Schuyler Colfax.* New York, 1886.

HOMANS, JAMES E., *Our Three Admirals, Farragut, Porter, Dewey.* New York, 1889.

HOWARD, HELEN A., *War Chief Joseph.* Caldwell, Idaho, 1946.

HOWARD, O. O., and PARKER, ELY S., *Some Reminiscences of Grant.* McClure's Magazine, May, 1894.

HOWE, HENRY, *Historical Collections of Ohio.* Norwalk, Ohio, 1896.

HOWE, M. A. D., *The Life and Labors of Bishop Hare.* New York, 1913.

HOWLAND, EDWARD, *Grant as a Soldier and Statesman.* Hartford, 1868.

HYDE, GEORGE E., *Red Cloud's Folk.* Norman, Okla., 1937.

JOHNSON, R. U. and BUEL, C. C., (Eds.) *Battles and Leaders of the Civil War.* 4 Vols. New York, 1887.

JOHNSTON, JOSEPH E., *Narrative of Military Operations.* New York, 1874.

JONES, GEORGE R., *Joseph Russell Jones.* Chicago, 1964.

JONES, J. B., *A Rebel War Clerk's Diary.* 2 Vols. Philadelphia, 1866.

JONES, J. WILLIAM, *Personal Reminiscences, Anecdotes, and Letters of General Robert E. Lee.* New York, 1875.

Kansas Historical Collections.

KING, CHARLES, *The True Ulysses S. Grant.* Philadelphia, 1914.

KING, MATTHEW W., *To Horse.* Cheboygan, Mich., 1926.

LARKE, JULIAN K., *General Grant and His Campaigns.* New York, 1864.

LEE, FITZHUGH, *General Lee.* New York, 1961.

LEWIS, LLOYD, *Captain Sam Grant.* Boston, 1950.

LEWIS, LLOYD, *Letters from Lloyd Lewis.* Boston, 1950.

Lincoln Lore. March, 1964, May, 1936, August 14, 1939, Fort Wayne, Ind.

LONGSTREET, JAMES, *From Manassa to Appomattox.* Philadelphia, 1896.

McCARTNEY, CLARENCE E., *Grant and His Generals.* New York, 1953.

McCLELLAN, CARSWELL, *The Personal Memoirs and Military History of U. S. Grant Versus the Record of the Army of the Potomac.* New York, 1887.

McCLELLAN, GEORGE B., *McClellan's Own Story.* New York, 1887.

McCORMICK, ROBERT R., *Ulysses S. Grant.* New York, 1950.

MEREDITH, ROY, *Mr. Lincoln's General: U. S. Grant.* New York, 1959.

MERINGTON, MARGUERITE, *The Custer Story.* New York, 1950.

MITCHELL, JOSEPH B., *Decisive Battles of the Civil War.* New York, 1955.

MONAGHAN, JAY, *Diplomat in Carpet Slippers.* Indianapolis, 1945.

Montana Historical Collections.

MOORE, FRANK, *The Rebellion Record.* 12 Vols. New York, 1864, 1868, 1869, 1871.

NEVINS, ALLAN, *Hamilton Fish: The Inner History of the Grant Administration.* New York, 1937.

NEWHALL, F. C., *With General Sheridan in Lee's Last Campaign.* Philadelphia, 1866.

NEWS LETTERS, *The Ulysses S. Grant Association.* Carbondale, Ill.

New York Commandery of Loyal Legion. New York, 1897.

New York Herald. July 17, 1876.

New York World. May 2, 1876.

North Dakota Historical Collections.

NYE W. S., *Carbine and Lance.* Norman, Okla., 1942.

OFFICIAL RECORD, *War of the Rebellion.* Washington, D.C., 1893.

Ohio Commandery of Loyal Legion. Vols. 1, 2, 3, 4, 5, Cincinnati, 1903.

OLSON, JAMES C., *Red Cloud and the Sioux Problem.* Lincoln, Neb., 1965.

OWENS, KENNETH N., *Galena, Grant, and the Fortunes of War.* DeKalb, Ill., 1963.

OWENS, WILLIAM M., *In Camp and Battle with the Washington Artillery of New Orleans.* Boston, 1885.

PAINE, BAYARD H., *Pioneers, Indians and Buffaloes.* Curtis, Neb., 1935.

PALMER, FRIEND, *Early Days in Detroit.* Detroit, 1906.

PERKINS, J. R., *Trails, Rails and War.* Indianapolis, 1929.

PHISTERER, FREDERICK, *Statistical Record of the Armies of the United States.* New York.

POND, GEORGE E., *The Shenandoah Valley in 1864.* New York, 1883.

PORTER, DAVID D., *The Naval History of the Civil War.* New York, 1886.

PORTER, HORACE, *Personal Traits of General Grant.* McClure's Magazine, Vol. 2, May, 1894.

PRATT, RICHARD N. (Edited by R. UTLEY) *Battlefield and Classroom.* New Haven, 1964.

PRUCHA, FRANCIS P., *Guide to the Military Posts of the U.S.* Madison, Wis., 1964.

REED, CAPT. W. I., *Letter to Colonel William Conant Church.* San Francisco, Aug. 25, 1909.

Report of the Commissioner of Indian Affairs to the Secretary of the Interior. Washington, D.C., 1866 through 1878.

Report of the Joint Committee on Reconstruction. Washington, D.C., 1866.

Report of the Joint Committee on the Conduct of the War. Washington, D.C., 1865.

Report of the Secretary of War. Washington, D.C., Aug. 12, 1867.

Report of the Special Commission Appointed to Investigate the Affairs of the Red Cloud Agency. Washington, D.C., July, 1875.

RICHARDSON, ALBERT D., *A Personal History of Ulysses S. Grant.* Hartford, 1868.

RINGWALT, J. L., *Anecdotes of General Ulysses S. Grant.* Philadelphia, 1886.

ROSS, ISHBEL, *Silhouette in Diamonds.* New York, 1960.

ROSS, ISHBEL, *The General's Wife.* New York, 1959.

RUSSELL, CHARLES EDWARD, *Blaine of Maine.* New York, 1931.

RUSSELL, CHARLES L., *Diary of a Visit to the United States—1883.* New York, 1910.

Sale of Post-Traderships. H. Rep. 144th Cong., 1st Sess. Report No. 799.

SCHURZ, CARL, *The Reminiscences of Carl Schurz.* 3 Vols. New York, 1913.

SEITZ, DON C., *The Dreadful Decade.* Indianapolis, 1926.

SHERIDAN, P. H., *Personal Memoirs of P. H. Sheridan.* 2 Vols. New York, 1888.

SHERMAN, JOHN, *John Sherman's Recollections of Forty Years in the House, Senate and Cabinet.* 2 Vols., Chicago, 1895.

SHERMAN, W. T., *Memoirs of Gen. W. T. Sherman.* 2 Vols., New York, 1891.

SIMON, JOHN J., *Ulysses S. Grant Chronology.* Columbus, 1963.

SIMPLOT, ALEX, *General Grant and the Incident at Dover.* Tradition Magazine, Apr., 1962.

South Dakota Historical Collections.

STARR, LOUIS M., *Reporting the Civil War.* New York, 1962.

STERN, PHILIP VAN DOREN, *They Were There.* New York, 1959.

STERN, PHILIP VAN DOREN, *When the Guns Roared.* Garden City, N.Y., 1965.

STEWART, EDGAR I., *Custer's Luck.* Norman, Okla., 1955.

TAUSSIG, WILLIAM, *Personal Recollections of General Grant.* Missouri Historical Society Publications, Vol. 2, St. Louis, 1903.

TODD, HELEN, *A Man Named Grant.* Boston, 1940.

Trial of William W. Belknap. Proceedings of the Senate, 44th Cong., 1st Sess., Washington, D.C., 1876.

TRINKA, ZENA I., *Out Where The West Begins.* St. Paul, 1920.

TROW, JOHN F., *Regulations for the U.S. Military Academy.* New York, 1857.

TUCKER, GLENN, *Hancock The Superb.* Indianapolis, 1960.

TURNER, KATHERINE C., *Redmen Calling on the Great White Father.* Norman, Okla., 1951.

UTLEY, ROBERT M., *Custer and the Great Controversy.* Los Angeles, 1962.

UTLEY, ROBERT M., *The Celebrated Peace Policy of General Grant.* North Dakota History, July, 1953.

WALKER, FRANCIS A., *History of the Second Army Corps.* New York, 1886.

WALLACE, WILLARD, *Soul of the Lion.* New York, 1960.

WAYLAND, JOHN W., *A History of Shenandoah County, Virginia.* Strasburg, Va., 1927.

WELLES, GIDEON, *Diary of Gideon Welles.* 3 Vols., New York, 1911.

WHITE, A. R., *The Blue and The Gray.* The American Educational League, 1898.

WILCOX, CADMUS M., *History of the Mexican War.* Washington, D.C., 1892.

WILLIAMSON, JAMES J., *Mosby's Rangers.* New York, 1909.

WILSON, JAMES H., *The Life of John Rawlins.* New York, 1916.

WISE, JENNINGS C., *The Red Man in the New World Drama.* Washington, D.C., 1931.

WISTER, OWEN, *Ulysses S. Grant.* Boston, 1900.

WOODWARD, W. E., *Meet General Grant.* New York, 1928.

YOUNG, JOHN RUSSELL, *Around the World with General Grant.* 2 Vols. New York, 1879.

INDEX